GW00360953

WELSH SHIPPING
FORGOTTEN FLEETS

WELSH SHIPPING
FORGOTTEN FLEETS

by

P. M. HEATON

THE STARLING PRESS LTD
PRINTERS & PUBLISHERS
RISCA   NEWPORT   GWENT
GREAT BRITAIN
1989

ISBN 1 872006 00 0

© First Edition June, 1989: P. M. Heaton

Published by P. M. Heaton, Abergavenny, Gwent, NP7 5PR

Printed by the Starling Press Ltd., Risca, Newport, Gwent, NP1 6YB

AUTHOR

Paul Michael Heaton was born at New Inn, Pontypool, in 1944 and was educated at Greenlawn Junior School in New Inn and the Wern Secondary School at Sebastopol. At fifteen he left school and commenced employment, at first in a local store and then with a builders' merchant. A year later he was appointed as a Deck Cadet in the Merchant Navy, with the Lamport and Holt Line of Liverpool, and served in their vessels *Chatham*, *Constable* and *Romney* usually in the Brazil and River Plate trades. He joined the Monmouthshire Constabulary (now Gwent) in 1963 and has served at Abergavenny, Cwmbran, Newport, the Traffic Department and as the Force Public Relations Officer, and is currently the Inspector's Representative for Wales on the Joint Central Committee of the Police Federation.

He has always maintained an interest in maritime history, and has had the following books published:

Reardon Smith 1905-1980
The Redbrook: A Deep-Sea Tramp
The Usk Ships
The Abbey Line
Reardon Smith Line
The South American Saint Line
Welsh Blockade Runners in the Spanish Civil War
Lamport & Holt
Tatems of Cardiff
Booth Line
Jack Billmeir Merchant Shipowner
The Baron Glanely of St. Fagans and W. J. Tatem Ltd. (with H. S. Appleyard)
Kaye, Son & Co. Ltd. (with K. O'Donoghue)

ACKNOWLEDGEMENTS

I would like to thank all those who have helped in the compilation of this volume, particularly:—

Marjorie, Lady Leighton of St. Mellons, J.P.

Mr. E. N. Taylor, Gosport

Mr. D. A. Burrell, Muirkirk

Mr. A. Duncan, Gravesend

Mr. T. Rayner, Ryde, Isle of Wight

Mr. J. D. Brown, Cardiff

Dr. D. J. Anderson, Cardiff

Mr. A. H. Lovering, Cardiff

Mr. H. S. Appleyard, Sunderland

Mr. John Lingwood, Sunderland

Mr. C. J. M. Carter, Wirral

Mr. Laurence Dunn, Gravesend

Mr. K. O'Donoghue, Gravesend

Mr. W. Clay, Bridgend

Mr. L. Pardoe-Thomas, Newport

Newport Harbour Commissioners

World Ship Society

Skyfotos Ltd., New Romney, Kent

The National Museum of Wales—Welsh Industrial and Maritime Museum, Cardiff

Cardiff Central, Newport and Cwmbran Reference Libraries.

CONTENTS

LIST OF ILLUSTRATIONS

27. Bought in 1953 the 'Liberty' ship "Dayrose" (2) was the last vessel to join the fleet. *(Skyfotos Ltd.)*
28. The motor coaster "Cornel" was built in Holland in 1938 for Lovering and Sons Ltd. *(Skyfotos Ltd.)*
29. The "Empire Punch" was acquired from the Ministry of War Transport in 1947. *(Skyfotos Ltd.)*
30. The war built coaster "Fennel" joined the Lovering fleet during 1948. *(Skyfotos Ltd.)*
31. The American built "Staniel" was bought by Lovering and Sons Ltd in 1949. *(Skyfotos Ltd.)*
32. The "Petertown" of 1938 was acquired by Lovering's in 1951. She was the last vessel to join the fleet. *(Skyfotos Ltd.)*

INTRODUCTION

The heyday of the South Wales tramp steamer has long since passed. In 1920 there were 122 shipping companies in Cardiff alone, owning 1.5 million tons of shipping. At that time Cardiff was the greatest shipping centre in the world. In his book *History of the Port of Cardiff* E. L. Chappell commented:—

> Ship owning at Cardiff developed from a business to a craze. The port became the centre of a great shipping boom which attracted millions of pounds from investors and speculators in all parts of the United Kingdom.

This was a reflection of Cardiff's position as the world's biggest coal exporting port, which had peaked in 1913 with shipments of 10½ million tons. Neither of these figures was to be repeated. Coal shipments fell following the First World War as the use of oil as a means of energy increased. With this fall the number of shipping companies also dwindled, until in 1989 there are but two left.

For a number of years I have been researching and recording the histories of a number of South Wales shipping ventures, many of which have been produced in the magazine *Sea Breezes* whilst others have formed the subject of books. However a number of these ventures, by the very nature of the material available would never individually fill the covers of a single volume, and as a result I decided to combine five of the most interesting ventures into one book. The material has been used before, but I am sure readers will agree, is well worth producing in this format as a record of the enterprise shown in five individual businesses.

Included are three shipping companies which operated ships tramping in world-markets, whilst another is devoted to a venture which specialised in the intermediate trades and as operators of Admiralty colliers. Finally the history of a small company operating in the coastal trades is covered. Four Cardiff and one Newport based venture are recorded.

I hope readers enjoy the contents of this book which sets out to give some idea of the enterprise which was present in the South Wales ports not that many years ago.

P. M. Heaton
June, 1989.

PART 1

CARDIFF'S DUNCAN SISTERS

J. T. DUNCAN AND COMPANY, CARDIFF

John Thomas Duncan, the son of a printer, was born at Glasgow on July 7, 1855. In his youth his family moved to Plymouth where he commenced his training as a shipbroker, thereafter serving as such for a short period at Cherbourg, before arriving at Cardiff, where he took up employment in the offices of Edward Earl and Company.

Cardiff had become the greatest coal exporting port in the world, and in these circumstances in 1883 he became established on his own account as a shipbroker. In 1889 he decided that the time was opportune to enter shipowning, and on December 18 of that year entered into partnership with a Frenchman, Jacques Victor Valette, under the title of Duncan, Valette and Company.

They negotiated the purchase of the steamer *Benefactor* from J. Hoult of Liverpool at a cost of £11,000, and registered her without change of name, in the ownership of a single ship company, the Benefactor Steamship Co. Ltd., of which the partnership became managers. The transaction took place on December 24, although they did not take delivery of the *Benefactor* until a week later on December 31, following her arrival from Gibraltar. This ship of 1,034 gross tons had been built in 1880 by W. H. Potter and Son of Liverpool.

M. Valette was the Cardiff agent to the French coal brokers Cie. Blanzdy Ouest, and although remaining more of a silent partner was nonetheless well placed to ensure regular and profitable employment for the ship in the coal trade from South Wales to French Channel and Bay of Biscay ports. From the beginning Mr. Duncan's brother-in-law, William Barclay Brown, who arrived in Cardiff from Glasgow in 1889, was appointed accountant to the partners. Initially the offices of the firm were at Mercantile Chambers, James Street, Cardiff, but in February, 1924 they moved to Portfield House, Adelaide Street, Cardiff.

In addition to his interest in Duncan, Valette and Company, Mr. Duncan took shares in a number of single ship companies managed by others, as follows: on November 26, 1889 he acquired three shares in the Ingleby Steamship Co. Ltd. at a cost of £189..9s..0d. On January 21, 1890 he purchased a further three shares in this company at a cost of £189..9s..0d., and finally on May 1, 1890 took a further three shares of £200..2s..0d. The Ingleby Steamship Co. Ltd., which was managed by E. Harris and Company, of Middlesbrough, actually took delivery of the newly completed steamer *Ingleby* (1,786 gross tons) from her builders, R. Cragg and Sons, Middlesbrough in May 1890. At the same time he took a small shareholding in the J. Hoult steamer *Bendi* (3,518 gross tons) which was completed in March 1890, by Schlesinger, Davis and Company, Newcastle. Other ships in which an interest was held at this time were the *Moliere* and *Zephyr*. The effect of these shareholdings was to ensure the rapid expansion of the shipbroking and agency business, as Duncan, Valette and Company were appointed to represent all these vessels at Cardiff and other Bristol Channel ports.

Thus the business prospered, and Mr. Duncan sought to further expand, but his partner declined to allocate further funds to the venture, and in 1895 withdrew from the partnership. His place was taken by Henry James Edwards, and the partnership was reconstituted as J. T. Duncan and Company. However John Thomas Duncan and Jacques Victor Valette remained close friends until the latter's death in 1911, and it is interesting to note that Mr. Duncan's son Norman married M. Valette's daughter, and their son, John Norman Valette Duncan, who trained as a barrister, subsequently entering into commerce, became the chairman of Rio Tinto Zinc.

Following these new arrangements, later in 1895 the opportunity to expand was taken when a second steamer was acquired, the *Stokesley* of 1,047 gross tons, from H. Baxter and Company of Whitley, and without change of name registered in the ownership of the newly-formed Stokesley Steamship Co. Ltd. This ship dated from 1883 when she had been completed by R. Cragg and Sons., Middlesbrough, originally to the order of T. English of Leith. Thereafter the two ships traded without incident between South Wales and French ports.

In 1895 Mr. Duncan took a small shareholding in the Ras Steamship Co. Ltd., managed by Graham and Company, London, which in March of that year took delivery of the steamer *Ras Rowa* from the yard of Furness, Withy and Co. Ltd., West Hartlepool. Mr. Duncan was a very astute businessman, and invested in a number of other ventures not always connected with the shipping industry. In 1898 he took shares in the Roath Pavilion Co. Ltd., of Cardiff, and from 1894 his wife had held shares in the Vale of Glamorgan Railway Co. Ltd.

On January 1, 1898 he acquired 500 £10 shares in the newly established Shamrock Shipping Co. Ltd., of Larne, followed on October 21 of the same year, with 500 £1 shares. At the same time an agreement was entered into between the two firms whereby J. T. Duncan and Company became the agents at Bristol Channel ports for the Shamrock fleet, and indeed were responsible for fixing coal cargoes for their ships which were all employed in the trade from South Wales to French Channel and Bay of Biscay ports. However, the terms of this agreement only allowed for one Duncan steamer to be employed in this trade alongside the Shamrock ships. In consequence of this in that same year the steamer *Benefactor* was sold, and after a succession of owners she was broken up in Germany in 1920.

16

This left the steamer *Stokesley* trading in conjunction with the Shamrock fleet, and provided for a profitable period of trading to the mutual advantage of both concerns. The fleet of the Shamrock Shipping Co. Ltd. grew to such an extent that by the First World War it numbered ten ships as follows:—

Name	Year Built
Raloo	1898
Clonlee	1899
Glynn	1899
Curran	1900
Gransha	1901
Skeldon	1903
Moyle	1907
Slemish	1909
Trostan	1910
Divis	1883 (acquired 1910)

At about this time Reginald George Colle and Henry Walter Phillips Waller entered the company's offices. Both became involved in the business at management level in later years.

Prior to the turn of the century the partners had on occasions secured the *Stokesley* on time-charter to the Admiralty as a collier, coaling the fleet usually in home waters but occasionally venturing into the Mediterranean. While the agreement with the Shamrock Shipping Co. Ltd. did not allow for additional vessels in the trade from South Wales to French ports, the acquisition of ships for time-chartering to the Admiralty did not breach this. As a result in 1901 J. T. Duncan and Company took delivery of the steamer *Maywood* of 1,188 gross tons from the Ailsa Shipbuilding Co. Ltd., Troon, which was registered in the ownership of the Maywood Steamship Co. Ltd., and there after was placed on long term time-charter to the Admiralty, serving mainly the Home and Mediterranean Fleets. This first ship built specially to the company's order was named after Mr. Duncan's home, "Maywood", in Gordon Road, Cardiff. So successful was the new venture that in 1905 an additional ship, the *J. Duncan* of 1,939 gross tons, was delivered to the partners from the Ailsa Shipbuilding Co. Ltd. Registered in the ownership of the J. Duncan Steamship Co. Ltd., she was named after Mr. Duncan's wife, Jessie.

Two years later a fourth steamer, the much larger *Frances Duncan* (2,384 gross tons) was delivered from Palmer and Company, Newcastle. Named after his mother, she was placed in the ownership of the Frances Duncan Steamship Co. Ltd. With the arrival of this ship the fleet consisted of four vessels, three of which, the *Maywood, J. Duncan* and *Frances Duncan* were on time-charter to the Admiralty, and the *Stokesley* usually trading alongside the vessels of the Shamrock Shipping Co. Ltd.

February 1, 1911 saw the two partners John Thomas Duncan and Henry James Edwards being joined by two of the founder's sons, Francis Thomas Duncan, who was born in 1884, and John William Duncan, born in 1885, and by his brother-in-law, the accountant William Barclay Brown. However later in the same year Mr. Edwards died.

Further expansion took place in 1912 when two new steamers, the *Agnes Duncan* (2,500 gross tons) and the *Ethel Duncan* (2,510 gross tons) arrived. Both named after daughters of Mr. Duncan, they were registered in newly-formed single ship companies which took their titles from the names of the ships. The *Agnes Duncan* was built by R. Duncan and Company, Port Glasgow, and the *Ethel Duncan* by MacKay Bros. of Alloa. The *Agnes Duncan* was specially designed to enable her to coal the Royal Navy's battleships, with her holds in line with the bunker hatches of these warships. To facilitate this her bridge was placed amidships, and her engine space aft, this being quite an innovation at the time.

At this time, with a number of their ships being named after female members of the founder's family, the fleet became better known as the "Duncan Sisters".

With the arrival of these two new ships the *Stokesley* after 17 years in the fleet was disposed of to Norwegian owners. She had a long career thereafter until on December 22, 1951, as the Swedish *Daisy*, she was wrecked off Holman in the Baltic while on passage Sweden to Hull with a cargo of timber, after a creditable 68 years afloat. This left five ships, all on Admiralty charter, but J. T. Duncan and Company continued to fix cargo for the Shamrock Shipping Company's fleet from South Wales.

On August 14, 1913 the partners suffered their first loss, when the *J. Duncan,* on passage Penarth to Devonport with a cargo of steam coal, ran ashore at Tolpedn, Cornwall. Strenuous efforts were made to refloat her, but after eight days these were abondoned and she was declared a total loss. Fortunately there had been no loss of life. Without delay an order was placed with the Dublin Dockyard Co. Ltd., Dublin, for a replacement which was duly delivered the following year as the second *J. Duncan* of 1,832 gross tons.

At the outbreak of the First World War the fleet still consisted of five steamers of which two were lost during the period of hostilities as the result of enemy action, but fortunately without loss of life. The first casualty suffered by J. T. Duncan and Company was the steamer *Maywood* which on September 30, 1916 was mined and sunk off Le Havre. Surprisingly she had not been on Admiralty service at the time. Eighteen days later, on October 18, the modern steamer *Ethel Duncan* was torpedoed and sunk by a submarine off Noop Head, Orkney, while serving as an Admiralty collier.

18

Meanwhile in 1916 William Barclay Brown died leaving the management of the business in the hands of the founder and his two sons. Mr. Duncan, having been a widower for twelve years, in 1917 married Mr. Brown's widow, Janet Liddell Brown.

In 1917 the Shipping Controller appointed the partners to manage the requisitioned Norwegian steamer *Barbara* of 935 gross tons, which dated from 1900. However at the end of the war she was returned to her owners.

At the conclusion of hostilities the fleet consisted of three ships, the *Frances Duncan* (built 1907), *Agnes Duncan* (1912) and *J. Duncan* (1914) and although all three in peace-time continued to be time-chartered to the Admiralty, it was not thought necessary or wise to acquire additional tonnage in view of the reduction in the requirements of the Admiralty brought about by the gradual introduction of oil in place of coal to power the fleet, and indeed the contraction in the Royal Navy itself in peace time. Like the J. T. Duncan ships, some of those of the Shamrock Shipping Company were requisitioned as Admiralty colliers during the war, and following hostilities those vessels which survived resumed their place in the trade from South Wales to French ports, supplemented by the acquisition of new and second-hand ships. The partners as before, fixed cargo, and represented Shamrock's ships throughout the Bristol Channel ports. It should be mentioned that the firm also represented many others and in 1919 were appointed South Wales agents for the Crown Agents for the Colonies.

In the post First World War years Mr. Duncan's stepsons, Ernest William Brown, who was born in 1896, and John Duncan Brown born 1904, and Mr. Waller's son, Henry Walter Rhymer Waller, born 1902, entered the business, and in later years became directors and shareholders in the reconstituted concern. In the following few years Ernest was responsible for opening offices at Newport and Swansea. However on December 27, 1921 the founder John Thomas Duncan was killed in a riding accident, while hunting at Tetbury, Wiltshire.

By 1929 the three Duncan ships were no longer required by the Admiralty, and with the termination of their charters were placed thereafter in the trade from South Wales to French Channel and Bay of Biscay ports with coal, gradually extending further afield to Spain and Portugal. On one occasion the *Agnes Duncan* lifted a cargo of citrus from the Mediterranean. The Shamrock ships also extended their voyages, and indeed some units were fixed from North East coast ports.

On December 5, 1929 the *Frances Duncan,* twelve hours out from Barry with a cargo of coal for Rouen, foundered in very heavy weather off Land's End. As she capsized her crew had to jump overboard into the sea, and in the particularly bad weather sixteen were lost. The five survivors, including her master Captain Frederick Martin, were picked up by the steamer *Alice Marie*. This tragedy had taken place not very far distant from where the first *J. Duncan* had been lost sixteen years earlier.

The loss of the *Frances Duncan* reduced the fleet to two ships, the *J. Duncan* (2) and the *Agnes Duncan*, and to remedy this the steamer *Parkhill* was acquired the following year from Mathew Taylor of Methil. This ship of 1,823 gross tons, which dated from 1922 was built by C. Rennoldson of South Shields, and was registered by the partners in the ownership of the Frances Duncan Steamship Co. Ltd., and renamed *Maywood,* second ship to bear the name in the fleet.

By the depression of the early 1930s the level of cargo available for shipment from South Wales had fallen to such an extent that in 1931 the partners decided to lay up the three ships, the *Maywood* and *Agnes Duncan* at Barry Docks and the *J. Duncan* at East Dock, Cardiff. At this time it was decided to convert the partnership into a limited company under the title of J. T. Duncan and Co. Ltd.

In 1934 after three years laid up, the *Agnes Duncan* was sent to Penarth, where, following survey, she was sold to the Russians and renamed *Boug.* It is believed that she survived thereafter until the mid 1960s. Shortly after the *J. Duncan* and *Maywood* resumed trading, and by 1937 there had been sufficient recovery to warrant the acquisition of a third ship. As a result the steamer *Wynding* of 1,149 gross tons was bought from W. A. Souter and Company, Newcastle. This ship which dated from 1922 was built at Amsterdam by Verschure. In the Duncan fleet she became the *Stokesley,* second ship to bear the name, and was registered in the ownership of the Frances Duncan Steamship Co. Ltd. In the event she was to be the last vessel acquired by the firm. The name *Stokesley* is taken from a district of Middlesbrough.

At the outbreak of the Second World War the fleet still consisted of three ships of which one was to be lost during the period of hostilities as a result of enemy action. In addition a ship managed on behalf of the Ministry of War Transport was also lost.

Shortly after the war started the *J. Duncan* was requisitioned by the Admiralty as a commissioned collier, and served at Scapa Flow coaling ships of the Royal Navy. The first loss suffered by the company was the *Stokesley* which on April 24, 1940 was mined and sunk in the Thames Estuary when inward bound. Tragically there was a heavy loss of life.

However, later in the year the Ministry of War Transport appointed J. T. Duncan and Co. Ltd to manage a number of foreign flag ships which had been taken over following the fall of their country of origin. These were the French *Egee* which had only been completed earlier in that same year; the Danish *Fylla* and *Erika;* and Dutch *Algarve* and *Santa Lucia,* and the Polish *Kowel.*

On January 15, 1941 when undergoing compass trials in Barry Roads, the *Maywood* struck a mine, and was so badly damaged that she had to be beached at Barry Island. However following makeshift repairs she was returned to service to be employed thereafter at Loch Ewe, coaling merchant ships congregating in readiness for sailing in Russian-bound convoys.

During 1941 the firm were appointed to manage the newly completed motorship *Underwood* of 1,990 gross tons. This ship was built by Henry Robb Ltd., Leith, and was to have been delivered to the Union Steam Ship Company of New Zealand, as the *Port Underwood,* but on completion was requisitioned by the Government. She was destined never to reach her owners in New Zealand, as on January 6, 1944 she was torpedoed and sunk by an E-boat in the Western Approaches to the English Channel while on a voyage from the Clyde carrying landing craft for South Coast ports in readiness for the invasion.

In 1945 two ships were allocated to the management of the firm. They were the *Josiah P. Cressey* (1,791 gross tons) which dated from 1943 and was on bareboat-charter to Britain from the United States, and the *Empire Connah* which was originally the German *Charlotte Cords* captured by Allied Forces at Travemunde, and although managed by Duncan's for a short period, was later in the year allocated to Russia. The other foreign flag ships were returned to their respective owners, and the Duncan ships, following the war were placed back on commercial service for their owner's account the *Maywood* was sent for more permanent repairs to her damage which necessitated the renewal of all the plating on one side of her hull.

The coal trade from South Wales had virtually ended and in view of this the *J. Duncan* and *Maywood* were employed alongside the *Josiah P. Cressey* in carrying coal, when and where available, fertilisers to West Germany and timber homewards, and in general in the intermediate tramp trades. In 1947 the *Josiah P. Cressey* was returned to the United States, but with the decline in the coal trade it was decided not to acquire any additional tonnage to supplement the *J. Duncan* and *Maywood*. The agency business prospered during this period, but on August 27, 1953 Francis Thomas Duncan died.

Having served the company for forty-two creditable years the steamer *J. Duncan* was sold for breaking up, arriving at the yard of T. W. Ward Ltd., Milford Haven on June 4, 1956. Thus the *Maywood* was left trading alone in an age when the South Wales collier was a thing of the past, and by 1958 she was laid up at Penarth. Preparations were made for her to undergo a further survey, but industrial action at the ship repairers intervened and by the time this dispute had been settled the freight market had dropped making her return to service uneconomic. As a result in November 1959 she was sold to Belgian shipbreakers.

Although no longer owning any ships, the firm continued in business as shipbrokers and forwarding agents, but in 1963 John William Duncan and Reginald George Colle died, followed five years later by the death of Ernest William Brown, and in 1978 when the offices at Portfield House, Adelaide Street, Cardiff, were due for demolition to make way for a redevelopment scheme, it was decided to dispose of the company. So on September 1, 1978 the firm passed into the hands of its former Swansea agents—Stockwood, Rees and Co. Ltd. Thus the company, albeit under different owners, is still in existence in South Wales.

FLEET LIST

Name and Period in Fleet	Gross Tons	History
Benefactor 1889-1898	1,034	1880 built by W. H. Potter and Son, Liverpool, as *Benefactor* for J. Hoult and Company, Liverpool; 1889 to Benefactor Steamship Co. Ltd. (Duncan, Valette and Company); 1895 managers restyled as J. T. Duncan and Company; 1898 to Halmstadt Shipping Company, Sunderland, renamed *Halmstadt;* 1903 to H. E. Hansen, Norway, renamed *Ageroen;* 1914 to R. Blakstad, renamed *Ferro;* 1916 to Jacobsen and Company, renamed *Skjaereg;* 1920 broken up in Germany.
Stokesley (1) 1895-1912	1,047	1883 built by R. Craggs and Sons, Middlesbrough, as *Stokesley* for T. English, Leith; c1890 to H. Baxter and Company, Whitley; 1895 to Stokesley Steamship Co. Ltd. (J. T. Duncan and Company); 1912 to Akties Stokesley (Lundegaard and Stray), Norway; 1920 to H. Rachlev, Sandefjord; 1921 to J. S. Skargaard, Oslo; 1922 to H. R. Aas, Oslo; 1929 to H. Bratt, Gothenburg, renamed *Daisy;* 22.12.1951 wrecked off Holman in the Baltic, while on passage Sweden to Hull with a cargo of timber.
Maywood (1) 1901-1916	1,188	1901 built by Ailsa Shipbuilding Co. Ltd., Troon, as *Maywood* for Maywood Steamship Co. Ltd. (J. T. Duncan and Company); 30.9.1916 mined and sunk off Le Havre.
J. Duncan (1) 1905-1913	1,939	1905 built by Ailsa Shipbuilding Co. Ltd., Troon, as *J. Duncan* for J. Duncan Steamship Co. Ltd. (J. T. Duncan and Company); 14.8.1913 wrecked at Tolpedn, Cornwall, while on passage Penarth to Devonport with a cargo of coal.

Name and Period in Fleet	Gross Tons	History
Frances Duncan 1907-1929	2,384	1907 built by Palmer and Company, Newcastle, as *Frances Duncan* for Frances Duncan Steamship Co. Ltd. (J. T. Duncan and Company); 5.12.1929 foundered off Land's End, while on passage Barry to Rouen with a cargo of coal; 16 of crew of 21 lost.
Agnes Duncan 1912-1934	2,500	1912 built by R. Duncan and Company, Port Glasgow, as *Agnes Duncan* for Agnes Duncan Steamship Co. Ltd. (J. T. Duncan and Company); 1934 to Russia, renamed *Boug;* 1960s still listed in Lloyd's Register—no other details.
Ethel Duncan 1912-1916	2,510	1912 built by MacKay Bros., Alloa, as *Ethel Duncan* for Ethel Duncan Steamship Co. Ltd. (J. T. Duncan and Company); 18.10.1916 torpedoed and sunk by submarine off Noop Head, Orkney.
J. Duncan (2) 1914-1956	1,832	1914 built by Dublin Dock Yard Co. Ltd., Dublin, as *J. Duncan* for J. Duncan Steamship Co. Ltd. (J. T. Duncan and Company); 4.6.1956 arrived at Milford Haven for breaking up by T. W. Ward.
Maywood (2) 1930-1959	1,823	1922 built by C. Rennoldson, South Shields; laid down for G. Lamy and Cie., France; completed as *Parkhill* for Mathew Taylor, Methil; 1930 to Frances Duncan Steamship Co. Ltd. (J. T. Duncan and Company); renamed *Maywood;* 16.11.1959 left Penarth in tow for breaking up at Zelzaete on the Ghent Canal.
Stokesley (2) 1937-1940	1,149	1922 built by Verschure, Amsterdam, as *Wynding* for W. A. Souter and Company, Newcastle; 1937 to Frances Duncan Steamship Co. Ltd. (J. T. Duncan and Co. Ltd.); renamed *Stokesley;* 24.4.1940 mined and sunk near Nore Light Vessel. Thames Estuary.

24

PART 2

SEAGERS OF CARDIFF

W. H. SEAGER AND COMPANY, CARDIFF

William Henry Seager, the son of William and Mary Jane Seager, was born at Ilfracombe, North Devon, on March 13, 1862. In his youth his family moved to Cardiff where he commenced his training as a ship's chandler and subsequently on November 8, 1890 he married Margaret Annie, the second daughter of John Elliot, of Newport Road, Cardiff.

Cardiff had become the greatest coal exporting port in the world, and a considerable amount of shipping used the port; and in these circumstances in 1892 he became established on his own account as a ship's chandler with offices at 109, Bute Street, Cardiff.

With the connections thus gained he decided to enter shipowning and in 1904 formed the firm of W. H. Seager and Company. At the same time an order was placed with Craig, Taylor and Company of Stockton-on-Tees for the construction of a steamer to their own design. This ship, the *Tempus* of 2,981 gross tons, was completed in September 1904 and placed in the ownership of the newly formed Tempus Shipping Co. Ltd under the management of W. H. Seager and Company.

Tempus is the Latin word for time, and so the firm's system of naming their ships with Latin names was introduced. William Henry Seager took a large proportion of the shares in the Tempus Shipping Co. Ltd., the others being taken by many friends and associates, including Captain William Reardon Smith, who was to keep his holding until the delivery of his own ship, the *City of Cardiff* in 1906.

The *Tempus* was employed in the traditional trades from the port, to the River Plate, Mediterranean and the Black Sea, originally under the command of Captain T. Calver. After five years it was decided to acquire a second ship, and in consequence during 1909 they took over control of the Starcross Steamship Co. Ltd and its single ship, the steamer *Starcross* (2,823 gross tons) from J. Hoggarth and Company of Cardiff. This ship had been built in 1894 by Richardson, Duck and Company, Stockton to the order of the Starcross Steamship Co. Ltd., under the management of Anning Bros., Cardiff, and prior to 1900 had passed to the Penylan Steamship Co. Ltd. (Woodruff, Shillito and Company, managers), also of Cardiff, before arriving in Hogarth's fleet in 1902. She had carried the name *Starcross* throughout her fifteen years service, but on entry into the Seager fleet was renamed *Virtus*.

Such were the fortunes of the firm that in 1910 an order was placed with Craig, Taylor and Co. Ltd., Stockton, for another steamer, which was duly completed n March 1911 as the *Amicus* (3,695 gross tons). Further expansion took place during the following year, with two ships entering the fleet, while the *Virtus,* after only three years, was disposed of. The first of these was the steamer *Margaret Jones* (2,852 gross tons) from the W. and C. T. Jones Steamship Co. Ltd., Cardiff. This ship had been built in 1893 by J. Readhead and Sons, South Shields, and became the *Beatus* in the Seager fleet. The other ship was the *Loyal Briton* (2,259 gross tons) from Gibbs and Lee of Cardiff. This ship was renamed *Salvus* and dated from 1904 when completed by J. Blumer and Company, Sunderland.

Sold during 1912 to Greek interests, the *Virtus* was renamed *Aikaterini* and in 1915 became the Norwegian *Askelad,* but became a casualty of the First World War when on September 8, 1917 she was torpedoed and sunk by the German submarine *UC17* in the North Atlantic while on passage from New York to Havre. With the sale of the *Virtus* the Starcross Steamship Co. Ltd. was wound up, and thereafter all the ships under the management of W. H. Seager and Company were registered in the ownership of the Tempus Shipping Co. Ltd.

A further ship was acquired during 1913. This was the *Norfolk Range* of 3,054 gross tons, which dated from 1905 when completed by Irvine's Shipbuilding and Dry Dock Co. Ltd., West Hartlepool to the order of the Neptune Steam Navigation Co. Ltd., of West Hartlepool. Originally managed by F. W. Bolam, this company was taken over by Furness, Withy and Co. Ltd. in 1910. In the Tempus Shipping Co. Ltd. she was renamed *Campus.* No ships were acquired in 1914, but during this year the *Beatus* after only two years in the fleet, was disposed of to other British owners who, two years later renamed her *Sydney Reid.* In 1924 she became the Greek *Magda* and in 1927 went to Spain as the *Ignacia Aguao,* surviving until 1933 when delivered to shipbreakers.

Thus at the outbreak of the First World War the fleet comprised the following vessels:—

Name	Year Built	Gross Tons
Tempus	1904	2,981
Amicus	1911	3,695
Salvus	1904	2,259
Campus	1905	3,054

During the period of hostilities a further three ships joined the fleet, and altogether three vessels owned by the Tempus Shipping Co. Ltd., together with a ship managed on behalf of the Shipping Controller were lost as a result of enemy action.

During 1915 the firm took the opportunity of acquiring an additional vessel when the *Pennine Range* (3,426 gross tons) joined the fleet as the *Darius.* This ship had been built by J. L. Thompson and Sons Ltd., Sunderland in 1903, and came from the same owners as the *Campus* two years earlier.

28

The first ship to come into contact with the enemy was the *Salvus* which on March 10, 1917 was attacked by a German submarine off Southern Ireland, but survived when the two torpedoes fired at her missed. Not so fortunate was their pioneer ship *Tempus* which five weeks later, on April 19 was torpedoed and sunk by a German submarine 130 miles from the Fastnet, while on passage from Carthagena to Garston with the loss of one member of her crew.

During the early part of May 1917 a new ship, the *Fiscus* (4,782 gross tons) was delivered to the Tempus Shipping Co. Ltd. from Craig, Taylor and Co. Ltd., Stockton. No sooner had the company taken delivery of the *Fiscus* than she was attacked by a German submarine in the North Sea on May 13, but fortunately she escaped when the torpedo fired at her missed.

Exactly a month later, on June 13 the *Darius,* after two years in the fleet, was torpedoed and sunk by a submarine 210 miles South West from the Fastnet while on passage from Villa Ricos, Spain to the Tyne with a cargo of iron ore. Tragically fifteen members of her crew were lost. After a mere seven months in the company's service, the *Fiscus,* which had previously survived a submarine attack, was torpedoed and sunk on December 20, 1917 ten miles from Cape Ivi, while on passage from Barry to Corfu with a cargo of coal. During the action one member of the crew was lost.

During 1917 the Shipping Controller appointed W. H. Seager and Company to manage four ships on their behalf. These were the ex-German ships *Polalp* (1,517 gross tons/built 1891) and *Polbrae* (1,217/1896), the Norwegian *Halvard* (1,701/1902) and the Dutch *Tellus* (1,522/1904).

During February 1918 the company took delivery of a new ship, the steamer *Promus* from Craig, Taylor and Co. Ltd., which at 4,816 gross tons was the largest to enter the fleet up to that date. The final casualty during the war was the managed steamer *Polbrae* which on May 4, 1918 while on passage from Cardiff to St. Malo with a cargo of patent fuel, was torpedoed and sunk by the German submarine *U60* 1¼ miles from Sharpnose, North Devon.

At the conclusion of hostilities the company owned four ships, the *Amicus, Salvus, Campus* and *Promus.* In addition they still managed the three surviving ships for the Shipping Controller, but early in 1919 the *Halvard* and *Tellus* were handed back to their respective owners.

The years immediately following the First World War were marked with a period of great prosperity for shipowners, as markets neglected during the war were restocked by industry returning to peace time production. As a result tonnage was much in demand and freight rates rocketed to an all time high level. The price being paid for ships at this time was up to ten times that being offered immediately before the war. While the majority of companies involved in the tramp trades from South Wales rapidly expanded during this period, acquiring ships at these much inflated prices, William Henry Seager, with much foresight, decided that this happy state of affairs could not last, and in consequence disposed of three of their ships during 1919 when the price being paid was at its highest. In this way considerable capital was acquired which, as will be shown later, was conserved for the future expansion of the company.

The *Amicus* was sold to other Cardiff owners who renamed her *Portreath;* in 1932 she became the Greek *Theoskepasti* and in 1944 the *Cygnet* under the Panamanian flag. Thereafter she survived without incident until March 15, 1950 when she was badly damaged by a mine off the Terschelling Light Vessel, while on passage from Emden to Hull with a cargo of scrap iron. As a result she was found to be unworthy of repair and was broken up by Clayton and Davie Ltd. at Dunston-on-Tyne. Passing to the Town Line of London the *Salvus* was renamed *Johnstown* and in 1924 was back on the Cardiff register without change of name. During 1930 she hoisted the Latvian flag, but on September 29, 1933 she foundered eighty miles North West of Brest, while on passage from Barry to Algiers with a cargo of coal. The *Campus* had three British owners during the next five years, being renamed *Marshall Plumer* in 1919, and *Brookway* in 1921. However during 1924 she passed to the Japanese flag as the *Tsurugisan Maru* and survived thereafter until October 27, 1942 when she was sunk by an Allied air attack off Bougainville.

Having accomplished these transactions, a ship was acquired from other Cardiff owners. This vessel, the *Scatwell* (4,425 gross tons) had been built in 1911 by Bartram and Sons Ltd., Sunderland as the *Maisie* for the Laming d'Ambrumenil Steamship Co. Ltd. of London, and had passed to Harris and Dixon Ltd. also of London in 1917 who renamed her *Scatwell*. A year later W. E. Hinde and Company of Cardiff acquired her. No sooner had this ship joined the fleet, and before a new name could be selected for her, than the Cairn Line of Newcastle made an offer for her which yielded a profit and she passed to them without change of name. In 1928 she went to Greek interests as the *Antonis G. Lemos,* surviving until August 24, 1938 when she sank following a collision with HMS *Keith* in position 50 deg. N., 02 deg. 10min. W., on a voyage from Danzig to Buenos Aires.

William Henry Seager had many other commercial and social interests outside and within the shipping industry. During 1918 he was created a Knight Batchelor in recognition of the invaluable services he rendered to recruiting, raising War Loans and helping the fighting forces. He was the first Member of Parliament for Cardiff East and retained the seat for the Coalition Government from 1918 to 1922. He was a Deputy Lieutenant of Glamorgan, Justice of the Peace for the City of Cardiff, and in 1932

30

was elected High Sheriff of Monmouthshire. He also served as a director of the British Steamship Owners' Association, director of the North of England Protecting and Indemnity Association, chairman of Cardiff Pilotage Authority (a position which was further honoured when a new pilot cutter was named after his wife, Lady Seager in 1919), trustee of Cardiff Royal Infirmary, governor of Hamadryad Seamen's Hospital, representative for Cardiff Incorporated Chamber of Commerce on the Committee of Lloyd's Register of Shipping, member of Executive Council of the Shipping Federation, president of the Chamber of Shipping of the United Kingdom, president of Cardiff and Bristol Channel Shipowners' Association, president of Cardiff Chamber of Commerce, chairman of the Cardiff Institute for the Blind, and together with a number of South Wales shipowners served as a director of the Ropner Shipbuilding and Repairing Co. (Stockton) Ltd from 1919 until the yard's closure in 1925.

Sir William had four children, John Elliot Seager (born on July 30, 1891), William Henry Seager (born January 28, 1893), George Leighton Seager (born January 11, 1896), and Margaret Annie Seager, who married Major Charles Ellis Feneley, R.A., who was taken prisoner for five years in the Second World War.

Tragically William, the second son, was lost during the First World War when serving as a Lieutenant in the 10th Battalion of the South Wales Borderers. He was killed in action on February 7, 1916 at Neuve Chapelle. In memory of his son, Sir William had ten homes built for aged seamen and their wives at Cardiff which were free from rent and rates, and still stand to this day. The two surviving sons had also served in the war, Elliot as a Captain, also with the South Wales Borderers, and was awarded the Military Cross, and Leighton with the Artists Rifles. Both were to join their father in the management of the firm, and were also to follow their father in his example of service to the community.

Elliot was a deputy lieutenant, Justice of the Peace, Honorary Adviser on Ships' Stores to the Ministry of Food, Fellow of the Institute of Chartered Shipbrokers, Chairman of Cardiff Pilotage Authority, Chairman of the South Wales and Monmouthshire Discharged Prisoner's Aid Society, Chairman of Government Business Training Scheme for Wales, Chairman of Cardiff and Bristol Channel Shipowners' Association, President of Cardiff Institute for the Blind, President of the Publicity Club of Cardiff, President of Cardiff Incorporated Chamber of Commerce, Vice-President of Cardiff and District Employment Committee, Governor of Queen's College, Taunton; Member of Cardiff Local Marine Board; Member of Board of Management of Cardiff Royal Infirmary; member of the Cardiff Appeals Tribunal of the Ministry of National Insurance; member of the Welsh National Council of the Y.M.C.A.; Trustee of South Wales Federation of Boys' Clubs; Treasurer of the Charity of Sir David R. Llewellyn for Clergymen and Ministers; member of Priory for Wales

31

Headquarters Committee, Order of St. John of Jerusalem; K.St.J.; High Sheriff of Glamorgan for 1937-38.

Leighton was created C.B.E. in 1932, a Knight Batchelor in his own right on July 7, 1938, a Baronet on July 1, 1952, and Baron Leighton of Saint Mellons on January 25, 1962. He served as Vice-Lieutenant of Monmouthshire in 1957; High Sheriff of Monmouthshire for 1938; Justice of the Peace, Deputy Lieutenant; as an Underwriter of Lloyd's; Chairman and Treasurer of the National Liberal Party; Deputy Chairman of Mountstuart Dry Docks Ltd.; Director of Cardiff Channel Dry Dock Company; Barry Graving Dock Company, New Egypt and Levant Shipping Co. Ltd., Atlantic Shipping and Trading Co. Ltd.; Chairman of Cardiff Post Office Adivsory Committee, Port of Cardiff Employment Committee, South Wales Advisory Committee to the Unemployment Assistance Board, Hamadryad Seamen's Hospital; Chairman of Visiting Justices to Cardiff Prison; Director and Treasurer of the Royal Merchant Navy School; Member of General Committee of Lloyd's Register, Monmouthshire Agricultural Wages Committee; President of the Chamber of Shipping of the United Kingdom, Cardiff Chamber of Commerce, Council of British Shipping of the United Kingdom, Cardiff Chamber of Commerce, Council of British Shipping, Advisory Council of Ministry of War Transport; Chairman of Cardiff and Bristol Channel Shipowners' Association; Governor of Cardiff Royal Infirmary; Trustee of Kingswood School; Governor of University College, Cardiff; Member of Tramp Shipping Advisory Committee under the British Shipping Assistance Act, 1934; represented the Shipping Industry on the Board of Trade Advisory Council; Warden of the Worshipful Company of Shipwrights; Freeman of the City of London; Welfare Officer for Monmouthshire with honorary rank of Captain; served in the Secretariat of Lord Rhondda when Minister of Food; honorary advisor to Lord Privy Seal on Trade Mission to Canada in 1929; member of the British Delegation to International Maritime Conferences at Geneva in 1935 and 1936; and was a member of Monmouthshire Police Authority from 1953, alternating between Chairman and Vice-Chairman from 1960.

After the First World War the composition of the business was changed somewhat. W. H. Seager and Company was converted into a limited company as W. H. Seager and Co. Ltd., continuing to manage the Tempus Shipping Co. Ltd. and its ships. The ships chandlery interests were later placed under a new company, Seager's Shipping Supplies Ltd., and all other investments under Sir William Seager and Sons Ltd.

With the disposal of the three ships in 1919 this left only the *Promus* in the ownership of the Tempus Shipping Co. Ltd., but the firm were still managing the *Polalp* for the Shipping Controller.

During 1920 Sir William purchased the steamer *Fernfield* for his own account. This ship had been built in 1895 by Furness, Withy and Co. Ltd., West Hartlepool for the Fernfield Steamship Co. Ltd., of London, and had been managed by Frederick Woods. Later in 1920 Sir William transferred this ship to the Tempus Shipping Co. Ltd., and the following year she was renamed *Tempus,* the second ship to carry the name in the fleet. However in 1922 she was sold to other British owners who renamed her *Hannevig Brothers* and in 1924 she was transferred to the Norwegian flag. By 1926 she had become the Italian *Assunzione,* surviving thereafter for only two years as in 1928 she was broken up.

Meanwhile in 1921 the *Polalp* was handed back to the British Government for disposal. Thus from 1922 the firm were a single-ship company with the modern steamer *Promus,* and with their connections were able to keep her profitably employed in the worldwide tramp trades. Other companies not managed as wisely were not as well placed as W. H. Seager and Co. Ltd. to cope with the crash of the early 1920s, and indeed half of Cardiff's tramp fleets were to disappear in these difficult years.

Eventually world trade started to make a recovery, so much so that Sir William and his two sons decided that the time was opportune to invest some of their substantial reserves. As a result, in 1924 they placed orders for the construction of three ships. The first to arrive was the steamer *Amicus* (2) (3,660 gross tons) from the Northumberland Shipbuilding Co. Ltd., Newcastle during January 1925. She was followed in March by a sister ship, the *Campus* (2) (3,667 gross tons) from the same yard, and the larger *Beatus* (2) (4,885 gross tons) from the Ropner Shipbuilding and Repairing Co. (Stockton) Ltd., Stockton-on-Tees.

Seagers were well placed from 1925 to take full advantage of the upturn in trade with its higher freight rates, and they employed all four of their ships in the world-wide tramp markets. Not only were the company's ships seen in the River Plate and the Mediterranean, but they traded to Australia, New Zealand and the Far East.

Such were the company's fortunes that during 1927 orders were placed for the construction of a further two ships with the Northumberland Shipbuilding Co. (1927) Ltd., Newcastle. The first to arrive in the fleet was the *Fiscus* (2) in April 1928 followed a month later by the *Salvus* (2). Both were steamers of 4,815 gross tons. During 1928 the company's expansion was completed when they acquired the steamer *Nolisement* from Morel Ltd., Cardiff. This ship of 4,447 gross tons had been built in 1915 by William Gray and Co. Ltd., West Hartlepool. In the Seager fleet she was renamed *Darius* (2). Thus the company were in a position to cope with the rigours ahead, with their fine modern fleet which now consisted of:—

Name	Year Built	Gross Tons
Promus	1918	4,816
Amicus (2)	1925	3,660
Beatus (2)	1925	4,885
Campus (2)	1925	3,667
Darius (2)	1915	4,447
Fiscus (2)	1928	4,815
Salvus (2)	1928	4,815

During the depression of the early 1930s the company through careful management was able to keep some of their ships employed, and the laying up of vessels was kept to a minimum. However in 1933 it was decided to dispose of the two older ships. During this year the *Promus* passed to the Greek flag as the *Adamas,* surviving until February 8, 1943 when she was involved in a collision in the North Sea, and was so badly damaged that she had to be sunk by gunfire from her naval escort. The *Darius* also went to Greek interests, as the *Marika Protopapa,* and as such survived an explosion and fire on board at Casablanca during November 1946. In 1947 she passed to the Panamanian flag, and the following year was renamed *Polac,* being further renamed *Balboa* in 1954. She arrived at Savona for breaking up on May 27, 1959 after a creditable forty-four years afloat.

Thereafter freight rates improved, and the five ships were profitably employed by the firm. However Sir William and his sons felt that further expansion was inappropriate, and that their fleet was adequate for the conditions prevailing prior to the Second World War.

At the outbreak of war the fleet comprised five ships, four of which were to be lost as the result of enemy action. In addition of a ship managed on behalf of the Ministry of War Transport also became a war loss.

During the first year of the war the company were fortunate enough not to lose any tonnage, but on October 18, 1940 they lost two ships on the same day, when the *Beatus* (2) and *Fiscus* (2) which were both part of the Eastbound Atlantic Convoy SC7 was attacked by a pack of German submarines. The *Beatus* was torpedoed and sunk by *U123* and the *Fiscus* was similarly sunk by *U100*. Fortunately there were no casualties among the crew of the *Beatus* but tragically the master and 37 crew of the *Fiscus* were lost, there only being one survivor.

Two months later, on December 19, the *Amicus* (2) was torpedoed and sunk by the Italian submarine *Bagnolini* approximately 240 miles West of Blacksod Bay, Co. Mayo, Ireland, with the tragic loss of her entire crew of 36. The next loss was incurred five months later on April 4, 1941 when the *Salvus* (2) was bombed and sunk by German aircraft in the North Sea off Cromer. Thus the *Campus* became the only ship left in the fleet, but during 1941 the Ministry of War Transport appointed W. H. Seager and Co. Ltd. to manage the newly completed *Empire Ness* (2,922 gross tons) and *Ocean Vanguard* (7,174 gross tons). The *Empire Ness* had been completed by Lithgows Ltd., Port Glasgow, while the latter vessel had been built in the United States by the Todd-California Shipbuilding Corporation of Richmond, California. However later in 1941 the *Empire Ness* was transferred by the Ministry of War Transport to others to manage, and on September 13, 1942 the *Ocean Vanguard,* on passage from Suez to New York was torpedoed and sunk by the German submarine *U515* about seventy miles East of Trinidad, with the loss of ten of her crew and one gunner. This represented the last casualty suffered by the company during the war.

Meanwhile during 1942 the company were appointed to manage a further two ships on behalf of the British Government. These were the *Ocean Fame* (7,173 gross tons) recently completed by the Todd-Bath Iron Shipbuilding Corporation, of Portland, Maine, and the *Fort Tremblant* (7,128 gross tons) built by the Victoria Machinery Depot Co. Ltd., Victoria, B.C., which was on bareboat charter to Britain from the Canadian Government. The following year an additional "Fort" ship was allocated to the firm, the *Fort Brandon* (7,131 gross tons) which had been built by the Burrard Dry Dock Co. Ltd., Vancouver.

Meanwhile on March 10, 1941 the founder of the company, Sir William Henry Seager died three days before what would have been his 79th birthday. Thus the management of the business was left in the hands of his two sons, Captain John Elliot Seager and Sir George Leighton Seager.

At the conclusion of hostilities the company only owned the one ship, the *Campus,* but they still managed the three vessels for the Government. For the greater part of the war the firm had also managed the Swedish *Moldavia* and Norwegian *Iron Baron,* but these were subsequently handed back to their respective owners. During 1946 the *Fort Brandon* and *Ocean Fame* were handed back to the Ministry. But at this time the *Empire Noble* (7,125 gross tons) was acquired from the Ministry of War Transport, and renamed *Amicus,* the third ship in the company's history to be so named. She had been built in 1944 by Vickers-Armstrong Ltd., Barrow, and was a steamer.

With the arrival of this new ship, the *Campus,* after 21 years reliable service was disposed of. She passed to the Radon Navigation Co. Ltd., of London, who renamed her *Radmar.* On January 12, 1952 she stranded off the Hook of Holland on passage from Rotterdam to Savona with a cargo of coal, and although refloated was declared a constructive total loss, and on May 27, 1952 arrived at Bruges, Belgium for breaking up.

The following year it was decided to purchase the managed *Fort Tremblant* from the Ministry of War Transport, and she joined the fleet as the *Beatus* (3). The company thereafter set about trading the *Amicus*

35

and *Beatus* in the world tramp trades, and they were to be seen in many parts of the world in the succeeding years.

At about this time Sir Leighton's eldest son, John Leighton Seager (born January 11, 1922) was appointed a director of the shipowning interests, while his younger brother Douglas Leighton Seager, became involved in the non-shipping interests with Sir William Seager and Sons Ltd. In this way a third generation of the family entered the business.

During 1948 the Ministry of War Transport allocated the management of the "Liberty" ship *Samshee* (7,210 gross tons built 1944) to the company for a short period which included her delivery voyage back to the United States. Two years later W. H. Seager and Co. Ltd were appointed to manage the *Fort Highfield* (7,129/1943), *Hillcrest Park* (7,138/1944) and *Yamaska Park* (7,151/1944) for a few months while the British Government negotiated their sale to other owners.

On January 8, 1955 Captain John Elliot Seager, M.C., D.L., J.P., died, being survived by his wife, Mrs Dorothy Irene Seager, M.B.E., J.P. The late Sir William's widow Margaret also died during this year on July 6, at the age of 93 years.

Later in 1955, with the reduction in the level of freight rates it was decided to dispose of the *Beatus,* and in consequence she was sold to the Stanhope Steamship Co. Ltd. (J. A. Billmeir, manager), of London, for whom she traded as the *Stanland* until delivered to shipbreakers at Hong Kong in 1963.

Thereafter Sir Leighton and his son traded the *Amicus* alone, but during the difficult years in the early 1960s she spent long periods laid up at Cardiff. Her last voyages, were when she was brought out of lay up to trade between Cuba and China in 1962. However in the Summer of 1963 it was decided to dispose of her and she passed to Hong Kong owners as the *Leela* and in 1964 passed to Liberian interests as the *Pacific Fir,* surviving until February 6, 1968 when she was abandoned by her crew after developing a leak during a voyage from Mormugao to Osaka. She later drifted aground on Koto Soh, about 25 miles East of South Taiwan, broke in two and became a total loss.

Meanwhile on January 25, 1962 Sir Leighton had been created the first Baron Leighton of St. Mellons, but on October 17 of the following year he died at the age of 67 years, being survived by his wife Marjorie, Lady Leighton of St. Mellons, J.P. His eldest son John succeeded to become the second Baron Leighton of St. Mellons.

Having outlasted most of the South Wales family shipowning businesses, and having sold their last ship during 1963, it was decided to close the business. As a result the Tempus Shipping Co. Ltd. was wound up, and during 1964 W. H. Seager and Co. Ltd and its agency business was disposed of to T. T. Pascoe Ltd., of Cardiff, to form part of the Pascoe Group, and the offices at 108-109, Bute Street, Cardiff were closed.

Thus the Seager family's involvement in shipowning came to an end after 60 years, but the memory of this noteworthy Cardiff tramp shipping company remains for the leading position they held in the industry, and for the place all three generations of the family held in the local community.

FLEET LIST

Name and Period in Fleet	Gross Tons	History
Tempus (1) 1904-1917	2,981	1904 built by Craig, Taylor and Company, Stockton, as *Tempus* for Tempus Shiping Co. Ltd; 19.4.1917 torpedoed and sunk by German submarine 130 miles N.W. by W½W from the Fastnet, while on passage from Carthagena to Garston; 1 member of crew lost.
Virtus 1909-1912	2,823	1894 built by Richardson, Duck and Company, Stockton, as *Starcross* for Starcross Steamship Co. Ltd. (Anning Bros.), Cardiff; c1900 to Penylan Steamship Co. Ltd. (Woodruff, Shillito and Company), Cardiff; 1902 to Starcross Steamship Co. Ltd. (J. Hoggarth and Company), Cardiff; 1909 ship and company taken over by W. H. Seager and Company, renamed *Virtus;* 1912 to Pandeli Bros., Pitarus, renamed *Aikaterini;* 1915 to Thv. B. Heistein and Sons, Norway, renamed *Askelad;* 1917 to A/S *Aslelad* (Leif Bryde), Norway; 1917 management transferred to Chr. Christensen Jnr.; 8.9.1917 torpedoed and sunk by German submarine *UC17* in position 47.35N, 07.25W, while on passage from New York to Havre.
Amicus (1) 1911-1919	3,695	1911 built by Craig, Taylor and Co. Ltd., Stockton, as *Amicus* for Tempus Shipping Co. Ltd.; 1919 to Portfield Steamship Co. Ltd. (W. E. Hinde and Company), Cardiff, renamed *Portreath;* 1932 to B. G. Mavros and S. N. Mendrinos, Greece, renamed *Theoskepasti;* 1944 to Cygnet Steamship Co. Ltd., Panama, renamed *Cygnet;* 1947 to Cia. Naviera Punta Arenas S.A., Panama; 13.3.1950 badly damaged by a mine off Terschelling Light Vessel, while on passage from Emden to Hull with a cargo of scrap iron; found to be unworthy of repair and broken up by Clayton and Davie Ltd., Dunston-on-Tyne.

Name and Period in Fleet	Gross Tons	History
Beatus (1) 1912-1914	2,852	1893 built by J. Readhead and Sons, South Shields, as *Margaret Jones* for W. and C. T. Jones Steamship Co. Ltd., Cardiff; 1912 to Tempus Shipping Co. Ltd., renamed *Beatus;* 1914 to Reid Steamship Co. Ltd. (W. S. Reid), London; 1916 management transferred to Reid, Rigg and Thue Ltd., renamed *Sydney Reid;* 1917 management transferred to J. S. Rees and Griffiths, Cardiff; 1917 management transferred to T. H. Griffiths and Co. (Depot) Ltd.; 1918 to Bede Steam Shipping Co. Ltd. (Frew, Elder and Company), Newcastle; 1924 to E. N. Vassilikos, Greece, renamed *Magda;* 1927 to F. Fernandez Aguado, Spain, renamed *Ignacia Aguado;* 1933 broken up.
Salvus (1) 1912-1919	2,259	1904 built by J. Blumer and Company, Sunderland, as *Loyal Briton* for Gibbs and Lee, Cardiff; 1912 to Tempus Shipping Co. Ltd., renamed *Salvus;* 10.3.1917 attacked by German submarine off Southern Ireland, but escaped when the two torpedoes fired at her missed; 1919 to Town Line (London) Ltd. (Harrison, Sons and Company), London, renamed *Johnstown;* 1924 to Christopher Jones and Company, Cardiff; 1930 to K. Blau and Company, Latvia, renamed *Andromeda;* 29.9.1933 foundered 80 miles N.W. of Brest, while on passage from Barry to Algiers with a cargo of coal.
Campus (1) 1913-1919	3,054	1905 built by Irvine's Shipbuilding and Dry Dock Co. Ltd., West Hartlepool, as *Norfolk Range* for Neptune Steam Navigation Co. Ltd. (F. W. Bolam), Newcastle; 1910 company taken over by Furness, Withy and Co. Ltd., West Hartlepool; 1913 to Tempus Shipping Co. Ltd., renamed *Campus;* 1919 to Kelvin Shipping co. Ltd. (Hugh Hogarth and Sons), Glasgow; 1919 to St. David's Navigation Co. Ltd. (E. L. and F. P. Williams), Cardiff, renamed *Marshall Plumer;* 1921 to St. Mary Steamship Co. Ltd. (Williams Bros. (Cardiff)

		Ltd.) Cardiff, renamed *Brookway;* 1924 to Awanokuni Kyodo Kisen Kabushiki Kaisha, Japan, renamed *Tsurugisan Maru;* 27.10.1942 sunk by air attack off Bougainville.
Darius (1) 1915-1917	3,426	1903 built by J. L Thompson and Sons Ltd., Sunderland, as *Pennine Range* for Neptune Steam Navigation Co. Ltd. (F. W. Bolam) Newcastle; 1910 company taken over by Furness, Withy and Co. Ltd., West Hartlepool; 1915 to Tempus Shipping Co. Ltd., renamed *Darius;* 13.6.1917 torpedoed and sunk by German submarine 210 miles S.W. from the Fastnet, while on passage from Villa Ricos, Spain to the Tyne with a cargo of iron ore; 15 members of crew lost.
Fiscus (1) 1917	4,782	1917 built by Craig, Taylor and Co. Ltd., West Hartlepool, as *Fiscus* for Tempus Shipping Co. Ltd.; 13.5.1917 attacked by German submarine in the North Sea, but escaped when the torpedo fired at her missed; 20.12.1917 torpedoed and sunk by German submarine 10 miles N.N.E. from Cape Ivi, while on passage from Barry to Corfu with a cargo of coal; 1 member of crew lost.
Promus 1918-1933	4.816	1918 built by Craig, Taylor and Co. Ltd., West Hartlepool, as *Promus* for Tempus Shipping Co. Ltd.; 1933 to C. M. Lemos, Greece, renamed *Adamas;* 1937 to Adamas Steamship Co. Ltd., Greece; 8.2.1943 involved in a collision in the North Sea and was so badly damaged that she was sunk by gunfire from escort.
Scatwell 1919	4,425	1911 built by Bartram and Sons Ltd., Sunderland, as *Maisie* for Laming d'Ambrumenil Steamship Co. Ltd. (A. Laming and Company), London; 1917 to Harris and Dixon Ltd., London, renamed *Scatwell;* 1918 to Portloe Steamship Co. Ltd. (W. E. Hinde and Company), Cardiff; 1919 to Tempus Shipping Co. Ltd.; 1919 to Cairn Line of Steamships Ltd. (Cairn, Noble and Company),

Newcastle; 1928 to S. A. and P. A. Lemos, Greece, renamed *Antonis G. Lemos;* 24.8.1936 sank following a collision with HMS *Keith* in position 50.00N, 02.10W, while on voyage from Danzig to Buenos Aires.

Fernfield *Tempus* (2) 1920-1922	3,142	1895 built by Furness, Withy and Co. Ltd., West Hartlepool, as *Fernfield* for Fernfield Steamship Co. Ltd., (Frederick Woods), London; 1920 to Sir William Henry Seager; 1920 transferred to Tempus Shipping Co. Ltd.; 1921 renamed *Tempus;* 1922 to Hannevig Bros. Ltd., London, renamed *Hannevig Brothers;* 1924 to D/S Martha A/S (H. Hannevig), Norway; 1926 to R. Rizzuto, Italy, renamed *Assunzione;* 1928 broken up.
Amicus (2) 1925-1940	3,660	1925 built by Northumberland Shipbuilding Co. Ltd., Newcastle, as *Amicus* for Tempus Shipping Co. Ltd.; 19.12.1940 torpedoed and sunk by Italian submarine *Bagnolini* approx. 240 miles West of Blacksod Bay, Co. Mayo, Ireland, in position 54.10N, 15.50W; her entire crew of 36 lost.
Beatus (2) 1925-1940	4,885	1925 built by Ropner Shipbuilding and Repairing Co. (Stockton) Ltd., Stockton, as *Beatus* for Tempus Shipping Co. Ltd.; 18.10.1940 torpedoed and sunk by German submarine *U123* in the North Atlantic in position 57.31N, 31.10W, while on passage from Three Rivers to the Tyne as part of Convoy SC7.
Campus (2) 1925-1946	3,667	1925 built by Northumberland Shipbuilding Co. Ltd., Newcastle, as *Campus* for Tempus Shipping Co. Ltd.; 1946 to Radon Navigation Co. Ltd. (Radonic Ltd.), London, renamed *Radmar;* 12.1.1952 stranded off the Hook of Holland, while on passage from Rotterdam to Savona with a cargo of coal, refloated, but subsequently declared a constructive total loss; 27.5.1952 arrived at Bruges, Belgium for breaking up.

Name and Period in Fleet	Gross Tons	History
Darius (2) 1928-1933	4,447	1915 built by William Gray and Co. Ltd., West Hartlepool, as *Nolisement* for Longueil Steamship Co. Ltd. (Morel Ltd.) Cardiff; 1928 to Tempus Shipping Co. Ltd., renamed *Darius;* 1933 to P. A. Protopapas, Hydra, Greece, renamed *Marika Protopapa;* 1936 transferred to Panos Protopapas, Greece; 1940 J. Livanos and Sons Ltd appointed as managers; 11.1946 damaged by an explosion and fire at Casablanca; 1947 to Saint Joseph Tramp Shipping Company, Panama; 1948 renamed *Polac;* 1950 Santelmo S.r.l. appointed as managers; 1954 to Cia. de Navegacion Cocle S.A., Panama, renamed *Balboa;* 27.5.1959 arrived at Savona for breaking up.
Fiscus (2) 1928-1940	4,815	1928 built by Northumberland Shipbuilding Co. Ltd., Newcastle, as *Fiscus* for Tempus Shipping Co. Ltd.; 18.10.1940 torpedoed and sunk by German submarine *U100* about 120 miles West of Barra Island, in position 57,29N, 11.10W, while part of Convoy SC7; master and 37 crew lost, only one survivor.
Salvus (2) 1928-1941	4,815	1928 built by Northumberland Shipbuilding Co. Ltd., Newcastle, as *Salvus* for Tempus Shipping Co. Ltd.; 4.4.1941 bombed and sunk by German aircraft in the North Sea off Cromer in position 53.05N, 01.27E.
Amicus (3) 1946-1963	7,125	1944 built by Vickers-Armstrong Ltd., Barrow, as *Empire Noble* for Ministry of War Transport, managers—J. Langdon Rees Ltd., London; 1946 to Tempus Shipping Co. Ltd., renamed *Amicus;* 1963 to Southland Navigation and Commerce Ltd., Hong Kong, renamed *Leela;* 1964 to Fir Line Ltd., Liberia, renamed *Pacific Fir;* 6.2.1968 abandoned by her crew in position 22.37N, 121.42E, after developing leaks during a voyage from Mormugao to Osaka, but later drifted aground on Koto Soh, about 25 miles East of South Taiwan, in position 22.5N, 121.50E, later broke her back and became a total loss.

42

Name and Period in Fleet	Gross Tons	History
Beatus (3) 1947-1955	7,442	1942 built by Victoria Machinery Depot Co. Ltd., Victoria, B.C., as *Fort Tremblant* for the Dominion of Canada and bareboat chartered to the Ministry of War Transport, managers— W. H. Seager and Co. Ltd.; 1947 to Tempus Shipping Co. Ltd.; renamed *Beatus;* 1955 to Stanhope Steamship Co. Ltd. (J. A. Billmeir and Co. Ltd.), London, renamed *Stanland;* 1963 broken up at Hong Kong.

SHIPS MANAGED ON BEHALF OF THE SHIPPING CONTROLLER

Name and Period Managed	Gross Tons	History
Polalp 1917-1921	1,517	1891 built by O. A. Brodin, Gefle, as *Axel Johnston* for Rederiaktiebolaget Nordstjeman (A. Johnston), Sweden; 1900 To H. F. C. Arp (S. Oligard and Thoersen), Germany, renamed *Brietzig;* 1917 allocated to the Shipping Controller, managers—W. H. Seager and Company, renamed *Polalp;* 1921 to Rondo Steamship Co. Ltd. (H. H. Penman), London; 1922 to F. Marchese Pucci, Italy, renamed *Ascensione;* 1924 renamed *Nereo;* 1929 to Joh. Linde, Estonia; 1933 broken up at Newport by J. Cashmore.
Polbrae 1917-1918	1,217	1896 built by Neptun, Rostock, as *Marie Horn* for H. C. Horn, Germany; 1917 allocated to the Shipping Controller, managers—W. H. Seager and Company, renamed *Polbrae;* 4.5.1918 torpedoed and sunk by German submarine *U60* 1¼ miles from Sharpnose, North Devon, while on passage from Cardiff to St. Malo with a cargo of patent fuel.
Halvard 1917-1919	1,701	1902 built by J. Priestman and Company, Sunderland, as *Halvard* for Actieselsk. Halvard (Bruusgaard, Kjosterud and Company), Norway; 1910 transferred to Bruusgaard, Kjosterud Dampskibsakties; 1917 taken over by the Shipping Controller, managers—W. H. Seager and Company; 1919 returned to Bruusgaard, Kjosterud Dampskibsakties; 1922 to Lai Hing Steamship Co. Ltd., Hong Kong; 1924 to Hop Hing Steamship Co. Ltd., Hong Kong; 1934 to Hwei Tung Steamship Company, Chefoo, renamed *Hwai Choing;* 1950/51 deleted from Lloyd's Register having been reported as a war loss; No other details

Name and Period Managed	Gross Tons	History
Tellus 1917-1919	1,522	1904 built by Nederlandsche Scheepsbouw Maatschappij, Amsterdam, as *Tellus* for Koninklijke Nederlandsche Stoomboot Maatschappij, Netherlands; 1917 taken over by the Shipping Controller, managers—W. H. Seager and Company; 1919 returned to Koninklijke Nederlandsche Stoomboot Maatschappij; 1931 to L. Berengier and A. Giannoni, France, renamed *Sebaa;* 12.1942 taken over by Italy, renamed *Forli;* 17.3.1943 torpedoed and sunk by HMS *Splendid* off Punta Licosa, near Palermo.

SHIPS MANAGED ON BEHALF OF THE MINISTRY OF WAR TRANSPORT

Name and Period Managed	Gross Tons	History
Empire Ness 1941	2,922	1941 built by Lithgows Ltd., Port Glasgow, as *Empire Ness* for the Ministry of War Transport, managers—W. H. Seager and Co. Ltd.; 1941 management transferred to Witherington and Everett; 1942 management transferred to W. A. Souter and Co. Ltd.; 30.11.1944 sunk in collision with vessel *William Paca* near Terneuzen, in the River Scheldt.
Ocean Vanguard 1941-1942	7,174	1941 built by Todd-California Shipbuilding Corporation, Richmond, Cal., as *Ocean Vanguard* for the Ministry of War Transport, managers—W. H. Seager and Co. Ltd.; 13.9.1942 torpedoed and sunk by German submarine *U515* about 70 miles East of Trinidad, in position 10.43N, 60.11W, while on passage from Suez to New York; 10 crew and 1 gunner lost.
Ocean Fame 1942-1946	7,173	1942 built by Todd-Bath Iron Shipbuilding Corporation, Portland, Maine, as *Ocean Fame* for the Ministry of War Transport, managers—W. H. Seager and Co. Ltd.; 7.8.1946 chartered to Ropner Shipping Co. Ltd. under the Ministry of War Transport's Ship Disposal Scheme, and delivered at Avonmouth; 7.2.1947 to Ropner Shipping Co. Ltd., renamed *Firby;* 1955 to N. G. Kyriakides Shipping Co. Ltd., London, renamed *Irene K;* 1958 owners restyled as Winchester Shipping Co. Ltd., London; 1964 renamed *Winchester Queen;* 29.11.1966 arrived at Bilbao for breaking up by Hierros Arbulu.
Fort Tremblant 1942-1947	7,128	See *Beatus* (3) in main fleet list for details.

46

Name and Period Managed	Gross Tons	History
Fort Brandon 1943-1946	7,131	1943 built by Burrard Dry Dock Co. Ltd., Vancouver, B.C., as *Fort Brandon* for the Dominion of Canada, and bareboat-chartered to the Ministry of War Transport, managers— W. H. Seager and Co. Ltd; 9.4.1946 sub-chartered to Houlder Bros. and Co. Ltd under the Ministry of War Transport's Ship Disposal Scheme, and delivered at Bahia Blanca; 14.6.1948 to Laurentian Shipping Co. Ltd., Montreal, renamed *Laurentian Hill;* 1950 re-registered at London, and Coulouthros Ltd appointed as managers; 1951 management transferred to Fern Hill Steamship Co. Ltd.; 1956 to Monover Compania Nav. S.A., Liberia, renamed *Taygetos;* 1960 sold, renamed *Aegean Sea;* No other details—believed since broken up.
Samshee 1948	7,210	1944 built by Bethlehem Fairfield Shipyard Inc., Baltimore, as *Samshee* for the United States Maritime Commission, and bareboat-chartered to the Ministry of War Transport, managers Hain Steamship Co. Ltd.; 1948 management transferred to W. H. Seager and Co. Ltd.; 11.6.1948 returned to United States Maritime Commission and placed in Reserve Fleet; 8.1964 broken up at New Orleans.
Fort Highfield 1950	7,129	1943 built by Victoria Machinery Depot Co. Ltd., Vancouver, B.C., as *Yoho Park* for the Canadian Government, managers—Park Steamship Co. Ltd.; 1944 bareboat-chartered to the Ministry of War Transport, managers— Dalhousie Steam and Motorship Co. Ltd., renamed *Fort Highfield;* 1950 management transferred to W. H. Seager and Co. Ltd.; 1950 to Dartmouth Overseas Freighters Ltd. (Nomikos (London) Ltd.), London, renamed *Darfield;* 1952 transferred to Windsor Overseas Freighters Ltd.; 28.2.1954 stranded 10 miles North of Los Angeles Harbour, while on passage from New Westminster to Garston with a cargo of timber, subsequently refloated

Name and
Period   *Gross*
Managed   *Tons*   *History*

but declared a Constructive Total Loss; 11.5.1954 arrived at Terminal Island, California for breaking up by National Metal and Steel Company.

Hillcrest Park 1950	7,138	1944 built by United Shipyards Ltd., Montreal, as *Hillcrest Park* for the Canadian Government, managers—Park Steamship Co. Ltd.; 9.4.1946 bareboat-chartered to the Ministry of War Transport, managers—Capper, Alexander and Company; 22.10.1946 sub-chartered to Cunard White Star Line Ltd.; 1950 management transferred to W. H. Seager and Co. Ltd.; 1950 to Black Lion Steamship Co. Ltd. (Counties Ship Management Co. Ltd.), London, renamed *Bembridge Hill;* 1950 management transferred to Frinton Shipbrokers Ltd.; 1953 management transferred back to Counties Ship Management Ltd.; 1957 to Marproeza Cia. Nav. S.A., Monrovia, renamed *Elimarie;* 1965 sold renamed *Tai Fong;* No other details—believed since broken up.
Yamaska Park 1950	7,151	1944 built by Marine Industries Ltd., Sorel, P. Q., as *Yamaska Park* for the Canadian Government, managers—Park Steamship Co. Ltd.; 20.4.1946 bareboat-chartered to the Ministry of War Transport, managers—J. A. Billmeir and Co. Ltd.; 24.8.1946 sub-chartered to Novocastria Shipping Co. Ltd for two years under the Ministry of War Transport's Ship Disposal Scheme, and delivered at Cristobal; charter subsequently extended; 30.6.1950 management transferred to W. H. Seager and Co. Ltd.; 1950 to Yamaska Steamship Co. Ltd. (Ships Finance and Management Co. Ltd.), London, renamed *Yamaska;* 1953 management transferred to Lambert Bros. Ltd.; 1959 sold, renamed *Gunn;* No other details—believed since broken up.

J. T. Duncan and Company's steamer "J. Duncan" (1) wrecked at Tolpedn, Cornwall on August 14, 1913.　　(F. E. Gibson)

The "Agnes Duncan" of 1912.

Built at Dublin in 1914 the "J. Duncan" (2) served the company for forty-two years.

(Skyfotos Ltd.)

The "Maywood" (2) was acquired in 1930 and when sold for breaking up in 1959 was the last ship owned by J. T. Duncan and Co. Ltd.

(Skyfotos Ltd.)

The "Tempus" of 1904 was W. H. Seager and Company's pioneer vessel.

(I. W. Rooke)

Built in 1894 the "Virtus" was acquired in 1909. She is shown under her earlier name of "Starcross".

(York Collection)

Built by the Northumberland Shipbuilding Co. Ltd., Newcastle, the "Amicus" (2) was one of three ships built for the Tempus Shipping Co. Ltd in 1925.

(Welsh Industrial and Maritime Museum)

The "Beatus" (2) of 1925.

(A. Duncan)

Built in 1925 the "Campus" (2) served the company until 1946.　　(Welsh Industrial and Maritime Museum)

Dating from 1915 the "Darius" (2) was bought from other Cardiff owners during 1928.

(York Collection)

The "Fiscus" (2) of 1928 was torpedoed and sunk in the North Atlantic on October 18, 1940 on the same day and in the same convoy as the "Beatus" (2) was lost.

(A. Duncan)

The "Salvus" (2) of 1928.

(A. Duncan)

Built in 1944 the "Amicus" (3) was acquired from the Ministry of War Transport two years later. (T. Rayner)

The "Beatus" (3) of 1942 was acquired in 1947.

(Welsh Industrial and Maritime Museum)

Built in 1913 by J. Priestman and Co. Ltd., Sunderland, the "Satrap" was one of six ships built for Pardoe-Thomas and Co. Ltd., Newport, in the three years before the First World War.

(York Collection)

The steamer "Slav" was built in 1913 by J. Crown and Son, Sunderland.

(National Maritime Museum)

The "Slav" shown under her later name of "Llantwit Major".

(E. N. Taylor)

Built in 1929 by Lithgows Ltd., Port Glasgow, the "Knight of St. George" was one of eight ships ordered by Pardoe-Thomas and Co. Ltd. in the same series.

(E. N. Taylor)

The "Knight of St. Michael" of 1929.

(Robertsons, Greenock)

The "Knight of St. John" of 1930.

(Robertsons, Greenock)

Built in 1930 the "Knight Almoner" was, like her sisters, an above average vessel to be owned by a Welsh tramp shipowner.
(E. N. Taylor)

Laid down in 1929 for Pardoe-Thomas and Co. Ltd. as the "Knight Batchelor" the ship was completed in 1936 by Lithgows Ltd., Port Glasgow, as the "Cape Sable" for the Lyle Shipping Co. Ltd.
(Skyfotos Ltd.)

The "Daybreak" of 1925 was the first ship built to the order of the Claymore Shipping Co. Ltd.

(York Collection)

The "Dayrose" (1) was built in 1928 by R. Thompson and Sons Ltd., Sunderland.

(York Collection)

The management of the Fairwater Shipping Co. Ltd., Cardiff, and its single ship "Fairwater" of 1928 was taken over by the directors of Claymore Shipping in 1936.

(York Collection)

The 'Empire' ship "Daydawn" (2) was six years old when acquired by the Claymore Shipping Co. Ltd. In 1949. (Skyfotos Ltd.)

Bought in 1953 the 'Liberty' ship "Dayrose" (2) was the last vessel to join the fleet.

(Skyfotos Ltd.)

The motor coaster "Cornel" was built in Holland in 1938 for Lovering and Sons Ltd.

(Skyfotos Ltd.)

The "Empire Punch" was acquired from the Ministry of War Transport in 1947.

(Skyfotos Ltd.)

The war built coaster "Fennel" joined the Lovering fleet during 1948.

(Skyfotos Ltd.)

The American built "Staniel" was bought by Lovering and Sons Ltd in 1949.

(Skyfotos Ltd.)

The "Petertown" of 1938 was acquired by Lovering's in 1951. She was the last vessel to join the fleet. (Skyfotos Ltd.)

PART 3

PARDOE-THOMAS'
WHITE CROSS LINE

PARDOE-THOMAS AND CO. LTD., NEWPORT

The Newport, Monmouthshire, shipping and shipbroking business of Pardoe-Thomas and Co. Ltd was formed in 1910, however the family origins of the founder can be traced to Dinas Cross, Pembrokeshire. The family moved to Newport in about 1850 where they originally lived in the docks area of the town at Watch House Parade, Pillgwenlly. John Pardoe-Thomas, the founder's father, trained in his youth as a sailmaker, and sailed as such in the full rigged ships of Liverpool's Black Ball Line. The legend.has it that his mother had a premonition that his ship would be lost and as a result travelled to Liverpool and persuaded him to leave the vessel and return home, and apparently the vessel was subsequently lost with all hands.

Thereafter John settled down ashore, and went into business on his own account as a sailmaker with premises at 116, Dock Street, Newport, which after his marriage was also his home and where he brought up his family, which included three sons, William Christopher who was born in 1860, Bertrum (Bertie) born in 1869, and Augustine Bazey (Gus) Pardoe-Thomas. William was originally apprenticed to his father as a sailmaker, but after his father withdrew from the business to become a Pastor and found the Alma Street Baptist Chapel, he entered the local office of the well known Newcastle shipowners Stephens, Sutton and Stephens, as a clerk. It was with this firm that he gained his experience of ship management and eventually became manager of their Cardiff office. Bertie went to London where he also entered the shipping industry, entering the offices of Frank C. Strick for whom he founded their Persian Gulf service, and later transferred to Bucknell Brothers. He was widely travelled, and had gathered many connections in the Mediterranean, Middle East and North Africa. The younger brother Gus was apprenticed to a local ironmonger, but soon after emigrated to New Zealand; he later moved on to Canada, and in the First World War surprised everyone by turning up at Newport in the uniform of an officer of the Canadian Army whilst en route to France. After the war Gus returned to Monmouthshire, where he married a local girl and took up farming at Chepstow where he died in the early 1930s.

However, their father, the Rev. John Pardoe-Thomas had died in 1900 at 67 years of age.

In 1910 Bertie returned to Newport where he formed the firm of Pardoe-Thomas and Co. Ltd., with offices at the former family home of 116, Dock Street, and commenced trading as a shipbroker and agent. The family had by this time moved to Home Cottage, Daniel Street, Newport.

At the same time he also decided to enter shipowning, and in consequence placed an order with J. Priestman and Co. Ltd., Sunderland, for the construction of a steamer fitted with tween decks. This ship, the *Saracen* (3,272 gross tons) was completed in April, 1911, and was placed in the ownership of the newly established Ottoman Line Ltd., and under the management of Pardoe-Thomas and Co. Ltd. As with all ships delivered before the First World War she was given a name from the Ottoman Empire (or Middle East) with the prefix letter 'S'.

The *Saracen* was placed in the trade from South Wales to the Mediterranean with coal outwards, and returning to the Bristol Channel usually with iron ore. Bertie was well connected, and was able to ensure that the ship was profitably employed right from the start. The venture proved so successful, and with the increase in coal shipments from South Wales ports, he decided to acquire additional vessels to take full advantage of these excellent trading conditions.

In consequence orders were placed at the Sunderland yards of J. Crown and Son and J. Priestman and Co. Ltd for the construction of five sisterships, all being self-trimming colliers, which were designed to be suitable for the Mediterranean and Baltic trades as well as for service on time-charter to the Admiralty as fleet colliers when required. These ships were delivered as follows:— from J. Crown and Son came the *Sheba* (2,268 gross tons) in August 1912, the *Sharon* (2,278 gross tons) in February 1913, and the *Slav* (2,278 gross tons) in August 1913, all to the order of the Ottoman Line Ltd. From J. Priestman and Co. Ltd. came the *Satrap* (2,234 gross tons) in September 1913 and the *Simoom* (2,222 gross tons) in April 1914, both to the order of the newly established Trident Line Ltd.

The years before the war were the most prosperous in the history of the South Wales ports, and Pardoe-Thomas and Co. Ltd. were well placed to take full advantage with their fine newly completed fleet. In addition to this rapid expansion in the intermediate tramp trades a small coaster joined the fleet in 1913. This vessel of 144 gross tons had been completed in 1910 at Paisley as the *Nessie* to the order of Ailsa Craig Granite Quarries Ltd., of Glasgow. In the Pardoe-Thomas fleet she was renamed *Sambo* and was placed in the trade to Ireland from South Wales, taking coal outward and usually returning with potatoes.

Thus in a little over three years Bertie Pardoe-Thomas had built up one of the most modern fleets operating from South Wales. Immediately after the outbreak of the First World War the Canadian Government, who were anxious to obtain modern tonnage as colliers to their naval fleet, made an offer for the *Sheba* and *Sharon* which was accepted, and they were transferred without delay and without change of names. The *Sharon* did not survive for long as on November 9, 1914 she sailed from Sydney, Nova Scotia for Newport with a cargo of steel products and disappeared with all hands. However, the *Sheba* had a long career; transferring back to the British register in 1924 as the *Hillcroft,* she subsequently underwent numerous changes of ownership until in 1936 she was broken up under the British Government's Scrap and Build Scheme.

At this point it should be mentioned that a sixth collier had been intended to join the fleet, and was to have been named *Shamal,* but due to the outbreak of hostilities the order was cancelled.

The first loss suffered by the firm occurred, when on December 31, 1915, the *Satrap* sailed from Barry with a cargo of coal for the Admiralty and went missing with all hands. The Admiralty maintained that the loss must have been through marine hazard, but the founder believed that she was a war loss, as there had been evidence of an explosion being heard off the South Wales coast at the relevant time, which would indicate that she had been mined. A memorial plaque to the loss of the ship's company was placed in the Church at Manorbier.

In 1915 the Shipping Controller had transferred the 882 gross ton steamer *Walter Dammeyer* to the ownership of Pardoe-Thomas and Co. Ltd., who renamed her *Polzeath.* This ship had been built in 1911 to the order of the Lynn and Hamburg Steamship Co. Ltd., of King's Lynn. This company which dated back to 1889 seems to have had strong German connections by way of finance or its directors, as at the outbreak of war the ship had been seized as forfeit to the Crown. A further steamer, the *Polanna* (2,345 gross tons) which dated form 1893 was allocated to the firm in 1916. This ex-German ship had been sunk in September 1914 in the Cameroon River by a British cruiser, and was subsequently raised and repaired.

At about this time Bertie Pardoe-Thomas was joined in the firm by his brother William, who became a director and substantial shareholder. It is interesting to note that throughout the war Pardoe-Thomas and Co. Ltd. were responsible for the Agency of the Admiralty on the Cardiff Exchange, purchasing the substantial requirements of coal for the Grand Fleet. It is not surprising therefore that the firm's fleet with the exception of the coaster *Sambo* and the tween decker *Saracen* were all employed as Admiralty colliers throughout the war.

The firm lost their second vessel on March 25, 1916 when the *Sambo* foundered in the Bristol Channel whilst on passage from Swansea to Morlaix. Also during this year the *Saracen* was sold, passing to the Letricheux Line of Swansea, for whom she traded until December 26, 1917, when she was mined and sunk near Brest whilst on passage from Bilbao to the Clyde with a cargo of iron ore. The *Polzeath* and *Polanna* were transferred to other owners during 1917; thus at the end of hostilities the firm had only two ships left, the *Slav* of the Ottoman Line and the *Simoom* of the Trident Line.

The period immediately following the war was one of great prosperity for shipowners as markets neglected in war time were restocked by industry returning to peace time production and as a result freight rates rocketed. The two colliers came off Admiralty service and returned to the peace time pattern of trade, usually to the Mediterranean, but occasionally extending further afield. Indeed at the end of 1919 the *Simoom* under the command of Captain J. McConkey was to be found loading ground nuts in West Africa, as far up the River Gambia as it was possible to take the vessel. Unfortunately during this voyage a number of members of the crew were taken ill with fever and two fatalities occurred.

The Pardoe-Thomas brothers were shrewd to recognise that this prosperous period could not last, and noting that ships were changing hands at many times their pre-war value, decided to dispose of their last two ships, at what was to turn out to be the very height of the market. Thus the *Simoom* on arrival at Rochester from West Africa, was sold on February 4, 1920 to the Portfield Steamship Co. Ltd., of Cardiff, for whom she became the *Portgwarra,* trading as such until December 31, 1921, when she foundered 11 miles from the Maas Light Vessel, while on passage from Blyth to Rotterdam with a cargo of coal. Exactly two weeks after the sale of the *Simoom,* on February 18, the *Slav* was sold to the Sanderson Shipping Co. Ltd., of Cardiff. Thereafter she had numerous owners, surviving until February 21, 1945, when as the Japanese *Tairiku Maru* she was torpedoed and sunk by the American submarine USS *Gato,* in position 35.24N, 125.23E.

Thereafter the firm withdrew temporarily from shipowning but continued as shipbrokers and agents from their Newport office still at 116, Dock Street. However, considerable capital had been acquired by the sale of their fleet which the brothers decided to keep until better times.

Right from the start it was the custom at Christmas for the company to send a message of goodwill to the crews of all their ships, and to give each man an extra day's pay. The following is the message sent to the master of the *Simoom* on Christmas Day, 1919, and which was read out to the crew:—

> As has been our custom ever since we started business, and as a little evidence of our goodwill, we want to give one day's pay to each member of your crew, as a gratuity from us (to include yourself right down to the cabin boy), and as well we want you to give each man a decent dinner, and make things as comfortable as you can on that day. Also please receive our wishes (with our kindest regards to you and Mr. Shaw) and give same to one and all, that you may spend a very happy Christmas. We shall be thinking of you, and we hope we shall have your good wishes, as you have ours.
>
> (signed) B. Pardoe-Thomas, Director

In 1928, having been without any ships for eight years, it was decided to re-enter shipowning, and in consequence orders were placed for the construction of eight steamers. Whereas in the past they had been involved mostly with colliers for the intermediate tramp trades, these new ships were designed with deep tween decks and were suitable for cargo liner operation. At the time of their appearance they were thought to be very modern looking, with their short raked funnels which made them look more like motorships than steamers.

Six of the new vessels were sisterships of 3,800 gross tons, all delivered to newly established single ship companies as follows : From J. Priestman and Co. Ltd., Sunderland came the *Knight of the Cross* in May 1929 for the Newport Africa Line Ltd., *Knight of the Rose* in July 1929 for the Newport America Line Ltd., and *Knight of the Realm* in January 1930 for the Newport Argentine Line Ltd.; from Lithgows Ltd., Port Glasgow came the *Knight of St. George* in August 1929 for the Newport Normandy Line Ltd., *Knight of St. Michael* in October 1929 for the Newport Provence Line Ltd., and *Knight of St. John* in February 1930 for Newport Liners Ltd.

The later pair, which completed the eight ship order consisted of two larger ships, each of 4,400 gross tons, the *Knight Almoner* for the Ottoman Line Ltd., and the *Knight Batchelor* for the Trident Line Ltd., both from Lithgows Ltd. The former ship was delivered in July 1930, whereas, in the event, due to the sudden downturn in world trade, the construction of the *Knight Batchelor* was suspended whilst still on the stocks.

This second fleet were given names from the Holy Crusades, and the fleet became known as the White Cross Line. With the earlier fleet the house flag had been a blue ground with a white letter 'T' surrounded by an outline circle thereon, but with the new fleet the houseflag was a blue ground with a white cross thereon, both fleets sharing a black funnel colour. The Pardoe-Thomas family's religious background was clearly reflected in the placing in each vessel's saloon of a symbol of Christianity in the form of a prominent plaque on which was engraved the company's houseflag, a white cross, studded with five red roses on a blue field, surrounded by the inscription "God's Providence is mine Inheritance".

On completion, the four ships delivered by Lithgows Ltd were placed on mortgage from Bertie Pardoe-Thomas and James Shearer of Lyle Shipping Co. Ltd., of Glasgow. All of these ships were well found smart vessels which were usually employed in the trades to and from the East Coast of South America, but owing to the rapidly deteriorating conditions were often later to be found in the general world wide tramp trades. In order to keep in the closest contact with the market an office was opened at 48, Fenchurch Street, London, EC3.

In December 1929 the *Knight of the Cross* was found to be on passage from New Orleans to the Continent, and in common with the rest of the fleet, the following message was read out to the crew on Christmas Day, reviving the earlier custom:—

> In conformity with our custom and happiness, our Senior instructs us to send to all our ships' crews, from the master to the cabin boy, our best wishes for a Merry Christmas and a Happy New Year, and to mark the occasion, we have had the pleasure each year, of requesting each master, to give the men a good time on that day, in a sensible homely way, and tell them, when giving them our best wishes, that an extra day's pay is to be given to each man, as a little recognition from us of the feeling that should exist between owners, master and crew.
>
> (signed) C. George, Secretary, for Pardoe-Thomas and Co. Ltd.

With hindsight, it could be said that the ordering of this large fleet was ill advised, but who could have foreseen the difficulties brought about by the great depression of the early 1930s? A consequence of this was very poor trading conditions with low freight rates, which resulted in the laying up of all seven ships at Newport Docks.

In 1933 two ships were disposed of, the *Knight of the Rose* to the United Africa Co. Ltd., of Liverpool for whom she became the *Gambian,* and the *Knight of the Realm* to the Scindia Steam Navigation Co. Ltd., of Bombay. However the former ship was resold in 1936, also to Scindia. During 1934 the four ships completed by Lithgows, namely the *Knight of St. George, Knight of St. Michael, Knight of St John* and *Knight Almoner* were all sold to the Lyle Shipping Co. Ltd., of Glasgow, who placed them all in the traditional tramp trades. This left only the *Knight of the Cross* which was still laid up at Newport, but in 1935 she also passed to the Scindia Steam Navigation Co. Ltd., who turned out to own the three ships built at the Priestman yard. The *Knight Batchelor* was completed at last in March 1936 as the *Cape Sable* for Lyle's, who in the event owned all five Lithgow built ships.

Four of the ships which went to Lyle's were lost in the Second World War. The *Knight Almoner* was torpedoed and sunk on June 21, 1940 by the German submarine *U23* South of Iceland whilst serving as a "Q" ship for the Admiralty. On February 23, 1941 the *Knight of St. Michael* was torpedoed and sunk by *U95* whilst on passage from Hull to New York in ballast. During 1942 both the *Knight of St. George* and *Knight of St. John* were lost, the former ship falling victim to an aircraft attack on May 2, whilst in a Russian convoy, and the latter being torpedoed and sunk by *U660* on August 10, while on passage from Boston to Sydney, Nova Scotia. The *Knight Batchelor* served Lyle's until 1958, and survived for a further ten years under other owners before arriving at a Japanese shipbreakers yard. Of the three ships that passed to Scindia, only one was lost during the war, that was the *Knight of the Cross* which on April 14, 1944 was one of the large number of vessels heavily damaged in the *Fort Stikine* explosion at Bombay. The ship was actually lifted from the dock by the tidal wave that followed the explosion and was left across a transit shed and had to be broken up where she lay. This explosion rendered a thousand people dead or injured. The *Knight of the Rose* and the *Knight of the Realm* were both sold by Scindia in 1955 and 1956 respectively, and were broken up in 1964 and 1969.

With the disposal of this fine fleet the Pardoe-Thomas brothers retired from shipowning, and in consequence all the companies under their control were wound up. The offices in London and Newport were closed, the latter passing at first to Watts, Watts and Co. Ltd., then to Newport Pilotage Authority, and although still standing was empty for many years. Bertie had been suffering with a long illness, and died in March 1937, at 67 years of age. William lived to the ripe old age of 94 years.

Of the three Pardoe-Thomas brothers only William had a family, which consisted of three sons and two daughters. The three sons all trained with a view to their eventually joining the business, Leon for the office and administration, Leslie for Engineering Superintendent and Lancelot (Lance) as Marine Superintendent. The oldest, Leon died in 1959 and at that time was serving with the Department of health as a Civil Servant; his record included service in the First World War with the 4th Welsh Field Artillery in France and Palestine.

Leslie who was born on March 3, 1900, was apprenticed in his youth to the Alexandra Dock Company, Newport, but left to serve in the war with the Royal Welsh Fusiliers in France and the Irish Rebellion, returning after hostilities to finish his training as a marine engineer. Thereafter he served for a voyage with Clan Line, and then followed eight years with Royal Mail Lines on the River Plate service from Southampton, usually on the *Alcantara*. After this he came ashore and served as engineer to the Six Bells Colliery at Abertillery, and then for the British Aluminium Company at Newport. He served on Newport Borough Council for many years, becoming Alderman and also served as Mayor of Newport, Chairman of Newport Borough Police Committee, and as a Justice of the Peace. In 1971/72 he served as Chairman of Newport Harbour Commissioners, an office held by his uncle Bertie in the period 1918/20. Bertie had actually presented the Harbour Commissioners with their Chairman's chain of office.

Lance who was born on July 5, 1906 served as a youngster with the Newport Pilotage Authority for six months, then joined Messrs. Frank. C. Strick as a Cadet, serving as Cadet and Third Mate of the steamer

Shahristan for five years, and a further three years as Third and Second Mate on their *Arabistan* followed by a single but long voyage in the *Mokta*. In 1933 during the great depression he had to leave the company due to the laying up of most of the fleet, and joined Santon's the electrical people of Newport, where he served until the Second World War. Having been a member of the Royal Naval Reserve and holding a Master's Certificate of Competency he became a Lieutenant and after training joined his brother's old ship, now the Armed Merchant Crusier HMS *Alcantara,* which was part of the 10th Cruiser Squadron. He served in a number of theatres of the war, including for nine months as King's Harbour Master of Brindisi, and then in the Commander in Chief's staff in Northern Naples and later at Malta. Returning after the war he rejoined Santon's but at the time of the Korean War was called up and placed as a Flight Lieutenant in the Royal Air Force at Schewert and Vienna, thereafter returning, and serving with the Youth Employment Bureau at Newport until his retirement.

This then, is the story of the Pardoe-Thomas shipping interests, which ended in 1936. However, it is also a testimonial of three generations of the same family's service not only to the shipping industry, but also to the local community.

FLEET LIST

Name and Period in Fleet	Gross Tons	History
Saracen 1911-1916	3,272	4.1911 built by J. Priestman and Co. Ltd., Sunderland as *Saracen* for Ottoman Line Ltd. (Pardoe-Thomas and Co. Ltd.); 1916 to Letricheux Line Ltd. (Letricheux and David Ltd.), Swansea; 26.12.1917 mined and sunk near Brest, while on passage from Bilbao to the Clyde with cargo of iron ore.
Sheba 1912-1914	2,268	8.1912 built by J. Crown and Son, Sunderland, as *Sheba* for Ottoman Line Ltd. (Pardoe-Thomas and Co. Ltd.); 1914 to Canadian Government; 1921 to Sheba Ltd. (Canadian Government Merchant Marine Ltd.); 1924 to Manor Line (London) Ltd. (C. Angel and Company), Cardiff, renamed *Hillcroft;* 1924 to Portrush Steamship Co. Ltd. (McNeil and Jones), Cardiff; 1924 transferred to Portsmouth Steamship Co. Ltd. (McNeil and Jones), Cardiff; 1933 to Westbourne Shipping Co. Ltd. (G. N. McNeil Ltd.), Cardiff; 1935 offered for breaking up under the Scrap and Build Scheme for a proposed 2,300 gross tons/4,000 tons deadweight vessel from Burntisland Shipbuilding Co. Ltd., but nothing resulted; 1935 to Rising Sun Navigation Co. Ltd. (Walter Vaughan (Cardiff) Ltd.), Cardiff for £3,200 and then offered for breaking up under the Scrap and Build Scheme for proposed 2,060 gross tons/3,500 tons deadweight vessel from Burntisland Shipbuilding Co. Ltd., but nothing resulted; 1935 to Thomas Dunlop and Sons, Glasgow, for £4,050 and offered for breaking up under the Scrap and Build Scheme against *Queen Anne* (4,937 gross tons, built in 1937); 1.1936 to T. W. Ward Ltd. for £2,800 and subsequently broken up by them.

Name and Period in Fleet	Gross Tons	History
Sharon 1913-1914	2,278	2.1913 built by J. Crown and Son, Sunderland as *Sharon* for Ottoman Line Ltd. (Pardoe-Thomas and Co. Ltd.); 1914 to Canadian Government; 9.11.1914 sailed from Sydney, Nova Scotia for Newport, Mon., with a cargo of steel products and disappeared.
Slav 1913-1920	2,278	8.1913 built by J. Crown and Son, Sunderland, as *Slav* for Ottoman Line Ltd. (Pardoe-Thomas and Co. Ltd.); 18.2.1920 to Sanderson Shipping Co. Ltd. (W. D. Vaughan and H. F. Abell Sanderson), Cardiff; 1921 to Comptoir Charbonnier Marit. Soc. Anon. (Schellen's Shipping and Agency Company), Antwerp, renamed *Rubens;* 1923 to Morfa Steam Navigation Co. Ltd. (Jones, Doughty and Co. Ltd.), Cardiff, renamed *Llantwit Major;* 1933 to Dah Loh Industrial Co. Ltd., Shanghai renamed *Dah Loh;* 1937 to G. Stamatilatos, Athens, renamed *Karavados;* c1942 seized by Japanese in Chinese waters, and renamed *Tatriku Maru;* 21.2.1945 torpedoed and sunk by American submarine USS *Gato* in position 32.24N, 125.23E.
Satrap 1913-1915	2,234	9.1913 built by J. Priestman and Co. Ltd., Sunderland, as *Satrap* for Trident Line Ltd. (Pardoe-Thomas and Co. Ltd.); 31.12.1915 sailed from Barry for Naval base in the North with a cargo of coal and disappeared; 9.2.1916 Posted Missing.
Sambo 1913-1916	144	8.1910 built by Fleming and Ferguson Ltd., Paisley, as *Nessie* for Ailsa Craig Granite Quarries Ltd., Glasgow; 1913 to Pardoe-Thomas and Co. Ltd., renamed *Sambo;* 25.3.1916 foundered in the Bristol Channel while on passage from Swansea to Morlaix.
Simoom 1914-1920	2,222	4.1914 built by J Priestman and Co. Ltd., Sunderland, as *Simoom* for Trident Line Ltd. (Pardoe-Thomas and Co. Ltd.); 4.2.1920 to Portfield Steamship Co. Ltd. (W. E. Hinde and Company), Cardiff, renamed *Portgwarra;*

Name and Period in Fleet	Gross Tons	History

31.12.1921 foundered 11 miles WSW of Maas Light Vessel, while on passage from Blyth to Rotterdam with a cargo of coal.

Polzeath
1915-1917   882

3.1911 built by Sunderland Shipbuilding Co. Ltd., Sunderland as *Walter Dammeyer* for Lynn and Hamburg Steamship Co. Ltd., King's Lynn, Norfolk (A. L. Tassell); (this company was formed in 1889, and it seems that it had strong German connections, possibly by way of finance or its directors, and as a result in 1914 seized as forfeit to the Crown); 1915 to Pardoe-Thomas and Co. Ltd., renamed *Polzeath;* 1916 transferred to B. Pardoe-Thomas; 1917 to Shipping Controller, managers—John Cory and Sons Ltd. Cardiff; 1922 to R. M. Sloman, Junior, Hamburg, renamed *Margretha;* 1922 to H. H. Schmidt, Hamburg; 1926 to Turner Edwards and Company, Bristol, renamed *Teane;* 25.1.1928 sailed from Swansea bound for Oporto with a cargo of coal, passed Lundy on the same day and then disappeared.

Polanna
1916-1917   2,345

1893 built by Blohm and Voss, Hamburg, as *Antoina* for Hamburg Sud. Amerika Dampfshiffahrts Ges. Hamburg; 1897 to Woerman Linie Ges. m.b.H., Germany, renamed. *Anna Woermann;* 9.1914 sunk in the Cameroon River by a British Cruiser; subsequently raised, repaired and in 1916 to Pardoe-Thomas and Co. Ltd., renamed *Polanna;* 24.5.1917 to Clyde Shipping Co. Ltd. (W. Cuthbert), Glasgow; 6.8.1917 torpedoed and sunk by German submarine *UC40* 3 miles East of Whitby.

Knight of the Cross
1929-1935   3,857

5.1929 built by J. Priestman and Co. Ltd., Sunderland, as *Knight of the Cross* for Newport Africa Line Ltd. (Pardoe-Thomas and Co. Ltd.); 1935 to Scindia Steam Navigation Co. Ltd., Bombay, renamed *Jalapadma;* 14.4.1944 extensively damaged in the *Fort Stikine*

61

explosion at Bombay; the resulting tidal wave lifted her from the dock and dropped her across one of the transit sheds; subsequently broken up 'in situ'.

Knight of the Rose 1929-1933	3,865	7.1929 built by J. Priestman and Co. Ltd., Sunderland as *Knight of the Rose* for Newport America Line Ltd. (Pardoe-Thomas and Co. Ltd.) 1933 to United Africa Co. Ltd., Liverpool, renamed *Gambian;* 1936 to Scindia Steam Navigation Co. Ltd., Bombay, renamed *Jalamani;* 1955 to Avance Cia. Maritima S.A., Costa Rica, renamed *Athos;* 1960 to Union Commercial Steamship Company, Lebanon, renamed *Filia;* 1964 broken up in Italy.
Knight of St. George 1929-1934	3,807	8.1929 built by Lithgows Ltd., Port Glasgow, as *Knight of St. George* for Newport Normandy Line Ltd. (Pardoe-Thomas and Co. Ltd.); 1934 to Lyle Shipping Co. Ltd., Glasgow, renamed *Cape Corso;* 2.5.1942 torpedoed and sunk by German aircraft North West of North Cape, in position 73.02N, 19.46E, while in convoy, on passage from Hull to Reykjavik for North Russia with a cargo of munitions; of her crew of 44 and 12 gunners, 39 crew and 11 gunners lost.
Knight of St. Michael 1929-1934	3,807	10.1929 built by Lithgows Ltd., Port Glasgow, as *Knight of St. Michael* for Newport Provence Line Ltd. (Pardoe-Thomas and Co. Ltd.); 1934 to Lyle Shipping Co. Ltd., Glasgow renamed *Cape Nelson;* 23.2.1941 torpedoed and sunk by German submarine *U95* South of Iceland in position 59.30N, 21W, while on passage from Hull to New York in ballast; Master and three crew lost out of 37.
Knight of the Realm 1930-1933	3,865	1.1930 built by J. Priestman and Co. Ltd., Sunderland, as *Knight of the Realm* for Newport Argentine Line Ltd. (Pardoe-Thomas and Co. Ltd.); 1933 to Scindia Steam Navigation Co. Ltd., Bombay, renamed *Jalaratna;* 1956 to Oceanic Enterprises Inc., Panama, renamed *Mindi;* 1957, renamed

		Coral; 1966 to Lloyd Mediterraneo di Armamento S.p.A., Palermo, renamed *Corallo;* 1968 to Tigerma S.A., Panama renamed *Tiger;* 7.9.1969 badly damaged in collision with *Kopalnia Kleofas* in position S4.26N, 11.41E; towed to Zeebrugge; had been on a voyage from Durres to Gdansk with a cargo of bitumen; 1969 broken up.
Knight of St. John 1930-1934	3,807	2,1930 built by Lithgows Ltd. Port Glasgow, as *Knight of St. John* for Newport Liners Ltd. (Pardoe Thomas and Co. Ltd.); 1934 to Lyle Shipping Co. Ltd., Glasgow, renamed *Cape Race;* 10.8.1942 torpedoed and sunk by German submarine *U660* in position 56.45N, 22.50W South of Iceland, while on passage from Boston and Sydney, Nova Scotia to Manchester in convoy SC94 with a cargo of 3,979 tons of timber and 1,040 tons of steel; crew of 63 all saved.
Knight Almoner 1930-1934	4,443	7.1930 built by Lithgows Ltd., Port Glasgow, as *Knight Almoner* for Ottoman Line Ltd. (Pardoe-Thomas and Co. Ltd.); 1934 to Lyle Shipping Co. Ltd., Glasgow, renamed *Cape Howe;* 15.9.1939 requisitioned by the Admirality, converted into an anti-submarine "Q" ship and renamed HMS *Prunella;* 21.6.1940 torpedoed and sunk by German submarine *U28* South of Iceland; only 13 survivors.
Knight Batchelor	4,398	1929 laid down by Lithgows Ltd., Port Glasgow, as *Knight Batchelor* for Trident Line Ltd. (Pardoe-Thomas and Co. Ltd.); 1930 construction suspended whilst vessel on the stocks; 3.1936 completed as *Cape Sable* for Lyle Shipping Co. Ltd., Glasgow; 1958 to Pan Norse Steamship Co. S.A., Panama, renamed *Eastern Venture;* 1967 to P. T. Gesuri Lloyd, Indonesia, renamed *Gema;* 1968 broken up in Japan.

PART 4

CLAYMORE SHIPPING
OF CARDIFF

CLAYMORE SHIPPING CO. LTD., CARDIFF

Charles Leigh Clay was born in 1866 and was the youngest son of Henry Clay. The origins of the family can be traced to Derbyshire, where they were involved in banking and brewing, and from whence Henry moved in the latter part of the 19th century to take up residence at Piercefield Park, Chepstow, in South East Wales. As was the practise in those days the eldest son inherited the bulk of the family estate, and in these circumstances Charles, being the youngest had to set about making his own fortune. Cardiff in the late 1880s was fast becoming the coal metropolis of the world and he therefore entered into business on his own account as a coal exporter, trading as C. L. Clay and Company, with offices at Exchange Building, Mount Stuart Square, Cardiff. He built his home, "Wyndcliffe Court", at St. Arvans, near Chepstow, situated at the southern end of the Wye Valley.

Having been established as a coal exporter for many years, he saw the opportunities which presented themselves in shipowning, and as a result in 1919 founded the Claymore Shipping Co. Ltd. with offices at Merthyr House, James Street, Cardiff. The end of the First World War saw considerable prosperity for tramp shipowners as markets neglected during hostilities were re-established, and many invested at the height of this trading cycle. However, by June 1920 the crash came and took with it many of those who invested in shipping at the much inflated prices in evidence at the end of the war.

The new company, although established in 1919, did not in fact purchase any tonnage until the following year after the market had crashed, and when prices of ships had fallen. Thus in 1920 the Claymore Shipping Co. Ltd. acquired four ships. The *Pelica* (2,144 gross tons) of 1909 and the *Porthcawl* (2,406 gross tons) of 1915 were purchased from the Scarisbrick Steamship Co. Ltd., a company which was managed by Eldridge and Morgan who also had offices at Merthyr House. These ships were renamed *Clayton* and *Claymont* respectively, being an adaption of the founder's surname. The other two ships were in the course of construction to the order of the Shipping Controller and were completed later in the year for the company as the *Daybeam* (3,023 gross tons) by J. Blumer and Co. Ltd., Sunderland, and the *Daybreak* (3,102 gross tons) by the Blyth Shipbuilding and Dry Dock Co. Ltd.

The four ships were employed in the traditional trades from South Wales, mainly to the Mediterranean but also as far afield as the River Plate. Charles Clay was subsequently joined on the board of directors by Sidney Palmer Richard, Frederick T. Dewey, and by his eldest son John

Charles Clay. Frederick Dewey was perhaps better known for his later connection with Cardiff City Football Club of which he became chairman, while John Charles Clay, who was born in 1898 and later lived at Great House, Bonvilston, was better known for his ability as a cricketer, being a leading player with Glamorgan.

During 1924 it was decided to sell the four year old steamer *Daybreak* and order a new vessel to their own specification. As a result the *Daybreak* passed to Japanese owners to be renamed *Aikoku Maru,* trading as such until January 12, 1937 when she was wrecked off Cape Shakotam, Hokkaido, while on passage from Otaru to Shimidzu with a cargo of coal. With the sale of this ship the order for her replacement was negotiated with R. Thompson and Sons Ltd., Sunderland. The new ship, built at a cost of £64,000 was named *Daybreak* (2) and was completed in 1925 with a gross tonnage of 3,598, making her a more suitable ship for the River Plate trade, where she carried coal outwards from South Wales and grain homewards to Europe. This was the staple trade for the South Wales tramp shipowner. The business as coal exporters now trading as Clay and Company ensured that profitable employment was found for the fleet.

In 1927 the *Clayton* was sold to Swedish owners for whom she traded as the *Mongolia* until August 13, 1940 when she was mined and sunk in the Kieler Bucht when on passage from Gelfe to Oslebshaussen with a cargo of ore. With the sale of this ship an order was placed with R. Thompson and Sons Ltd., Sunderland, for a replacement, and this ship was delivered in 1928 as the *Dayrose* (4,113 gross tons).

During 1928 and 1929 it was decided, in view of the state of the freight market, to dispose of the two older ships. Thus the *Claymont* was sold to Norwegian owners for whom she became the *Loke*. She had a number of owners thereafter and had a long career until on April 11, 1962 she was posted missing on a voyage from Casablanca to Venice with a cargo of phosphate. The *Daybeam* passed to Spanish owners and survived until April 1968 when she was broken up at Istanbul.

Thereafter the company concentrated on trading the two modern units of the fleet, the *Daybreak* (2) of 1925 and *Dayrose* of 1928, and they were almost exclusively employed in the River Plate trade. The reduction of the fleet was timely in view of the depression of the early 1930s; the dividend of 5 per cent less tax for the financial year of 1928/29 on a paid up capital of £100,000 was to be the last paid for a number of years. The company made losses during the period, examples being as follows:—

Year ended 31.3. 1934—loss of £2,086.
Year ended 31.3.1935—loss of £607.

In the Annual Report for 1934/35 the following sums up the conditions:—
After referring to minimum homeward rates in the Plate trade the report points out that, "unfortunately, the amount of

outward business available is much less than is needed to balance the homeward trade—there is, consequently, keen competition for what outward freights there are, and the rates are correspondingly low.''

Poor trading conditions resulted in the sale of the *Daybreak* (2) in November 1934 for the sum £22,000. The ship passed to the Greek flag and was subsequently lost in the Second World War when on October 8, 1942 she was torpedoed and sunk by the German submarine *U68* South of Cape Race while on passage from Rosario to Beira via Table Bay with a cargo of maize; four of her crew of 31 were lost.

Thereafter the *Dayrose* traded as the company's only vessel. The most noteworthy event which occurred in the mid-1930s was the granting of a subsidy of £2m by the British Government to tramp shipowners. The payments to the Claymore Shipping Co. Ltd. under the Tramp Shipping Subsidy for the years 1935 and 1936 were £2,340..2s..0d and £2,166..6s..0d respectively. A subsidy was approved for 1937 but not paid due to a temporary upturn in the freight market.

In 1936 the directors of the Claymore Shipping Co. Ltd. took over the management of the Fairwater Shipping Co. Ltd., of Cardiff which owned the steamer *Fairwater* of 1928, a virtual sister ship of the *Dayrose,* having been built only a matter of months earlier at the same yard. The paid up capital of the Fairwater Shipping Co. Ltd. was £34,730 of which £14,000 was held by the Claymore Shipping Co. Ltd. The directors of the Claymore Shipping Co. Ltd. and the Fairwater Co. Ltd. now comprised Messrs. S. P. Richard (chairman), F. T. Dewey and J. C. Clay. Mr Charles Leigh Clay had retired from the business which he had founded and died during 1944 at 78 years of age.

Conditions improved somewhat during 1936 and 1937 and in the case of the Claymore Shipping Co. Ltd. profits of £1,763 and £15,956 respectively were recorded, resulting in a 5 per cent dividend less income tax being paid during 1937, the first for eight years. The Annual Report of the directors of the company for the latter year included the following interesting text:—

> Following six years of depression, the shipping boom rapidly reached its peak, and, after a career as brief as it was brilliant, collapsed last October (1937). Current freights do not cover running costs, and many ships have already been laid up. Whatever the future for shipping may be—and in these days of economic instability there may well be another boom around the corner—the boom of 1937 has ended. Its passing has left the industry to face the future with a burden and a prop—a burden of increased costs, and a prop of voluntary cooperation. Will the prop prove strong enough to support the burden, and

keep the industry afloat until foreign trade revives? If not, a renewal of the Government subsidy is surely inevitable, for the millions now being spent on national defence would be largely wasted unless they included whatever provision may be needed for the preservation of the merchant service.

The Fairwater Shipping Co. Ltd. made a profit for 1937 of £17,251, and again the following extract from the Annual Report is of interest:—

During the greater part of the year freights were good, and the S.S. *Fairwater,* running uninterruptedly in the River Plate trade, participated in the good business obtainable. The early autumn saw a sudden collapse of freight markets generally, and of the River Plate market in particular, so the S.S. *Fairwater* was sent to Burma to load for Europe. This voyage will shortly be completed, and should show a profit, but the prospects for her future employment are far from reassuring.

Quite as big a problem as the fall in freights has been the heavy increase in working costs. Wages, stores, insurances, repairs, bunker coals, in fact everything connected with a ship has gone up in price, so that the cost of running the S.S. *Fairwater* is today about 40 per cent more than it was two years ago.

The cost of building new tonnage has also risen at least 50 per cent, necessitating the provision of larger reserves for depreciation and replacement.

However, a dividend of 10 per cent was paid for the year, the first paid for ten years.

During 1939, to promote the building of merchant ships, the British Government approved the granting of loans to shipowners to build ships in British yards and the Claymore Shipping Co. Ltd. was granted a £75,000 loan under the Shipping Loan Act, 1939. As a result an order was placed with W. Pickersgill and Sons Ltd., Sunderland, for the construction of a steamer of 4,768 gross tons.

At about this time the company also acquired a 4,729 gross ton steamer, the *Seringa* from Chr. Salvesen of Leith. This ship had originally been the Reardon Smith Line's *Falls City* of 1913, and entered the Claymore Shipping fleet without change of name.

Thus at the outbreak of the Second World War the two fleets consisted of the *Dayrose* (1928), *Seringa* (1913), *Fairwater* (1928) and a fourth vessel under construction. Of these, two ships were lost as a result of enemy action, as was another ship managed by the company on behalf of the Ministry of War Transport. The ships, although managed by the Claymore Shipping Co. Ltd. and the Fairwater Shipping Co. Ltd., were controlled as regards cargoes and routing by the British Government. During 1940 the management of the Danish steamer *Soborg* (1,993 gross tons) which had diverted into Lisbon and subsequent British service after the fall of Denmark, was passed to Claymore Shipping.

The new ship, *Daydawn,* laid down at Sunderland on June 6, 1939 was launched on December 9 and finally completed on January 16, 1940, sailing from Sunderland three weeks later on February 8. She was however to be the firm's first loss when on November 21 of the same year she was torpedoed and sunk by the German submarine *U103* while on passage from Barry to Rio Santiago with a cargo of coal, in convoy OB244 with the loss of two of her crew of 38.

More fortunate was the *Fairwater* which had been attacked by German aircraft on July 4, 1940, and although bombed and gunned South East of Start Point she survived and following repairs was returned to service. The company suffered their second loss on January 14, 1942 when the 14 year old *Dayrose* was torpedoed and sunk by the submarine *U552* near Cape Race, while on passage from St. John's, Newfoundland to Halifax with the tragic loss of 38 of her crew of 42.

Meanwhile early in 1941 the Ministry of War Transport had placed the management of a new "Empire" ship, the *Empire Sky* in the hands of the Claymore Shipping Co. Ltd. This vessel of 7,455 gross tons had been built by J. L. Thompson and Sons Ltd., of Sunderland. Unfortunately on November 14, 1942 she was lost when torpedoed and sunk by the submarine *U625,* while on an independant sailing from Hull via Loch Ewe and Reykjavik to Archangel with Government stores. Tragically her entire crew was lost.

At the end of hostilities the Danish *Soborg* was handed back to her original owners, leaving the company with their own two surviving ships, *Seringa* (1913) and *Fairwater* (1928). However in view of the demand for tonnage immediately following the war the decision was taken to sell the two ships at a satisfactory price, in order to accumulate funds for the acquisition of more modern tonnage. The two ships passed into the ownership of the Basra Steam Shipping Co. Ltd., of London, a company managed by Galbraith, Pembroke and Co. Ltd. They were subsequently resold, the *Seringa* surviving until 1960 when she was broken up at Karachi, while the *Fairwater* was broken up a year earlier at Ghent.

No ships were owned by the firm for two years, but in 1947 they re-entered shipowning when a three year old "Liberty" ship was acquired. The *Samdonard* of 7,233 gross tons was a product of the Bethlehem Fairfield Shipyard at Baltimore, and had been bareboat-chartered by the United States Maritime Commission to the British Government. Placed in the Claymore fleet she was renamed *Daybeam* (2) and put into the general tramp trades which invariably meant to and from the River Plate.

The reduction in coal exports from South Wales often meant outward passages in ballast, but nonetheless some good returns were achieved.

Following a fire at Merthyr House, the business moved offices to 60, Mount Stuart Square, Cardiff. Unfortunately at about this time Mr. Richard died, his shareholding passing to his widow. The business was now being managed by Messrs. F. T. Dewey and J. C. Clay.

During 1949 a second vessel was acquired from the British Government. This ship was the *Empire Nerissa* which had been built at the Glasgow yard of Harland and Wolff Ltd. in 1943. She entered the Claymore fleet as the *Daydawn* (2) and was of 7,036 gross tons.

As a result of the world wide shortage of tonnage created by the Korean War, it was decided to dispose of the *Daybeam* (2) in 1952 after five years in the fleet. She traded thereafter for a further sixteen years before her arrival at Kaohsiung on March 23, 1968 for breaking up. A year after the sale of this ship, in 1953, it was decided to acquire a replacement. Thus another "Liberty" ship, the Dutch flag *Prins Willem II* (7,265 gross tons) was acquired. She dated from 1943 a product of the Permanente Metals Corporation of Richmond and entered the Claymore fleet as the *Dayrose* (2).

Again a year later, in 1954, coinciding with an upturn in the freight market and consequent increase in ship sale prices, it was decided to dispose of the *Daydawn* (2) after five years in the fleet. she traded subsequently until 1966 when she was broken up at Split. With the sale of this ship the Claymore Shipping Co. Ltd. was liquidated, and at the same time another company with the same title was incorporated with an issued share capital of £300,000. This enabled the shareholders to benefit from the capital obtained from the post war sale of the ships.

After this their sole ship, the *Dayrose* continued trading for the company, engaged in the world wide tramp trades. During 1956 at the time of the Suez crisis, and in view of the extraordinary prices being paid for "Liberty" ships of the class and excellent condition of the *Dayrose,* it was decided reluctantly, but wisely, to dispose of her in order to take advantage of these conditions. As a result she passed to Panamanian interests and after a subsequent change of ownership was finally broken up at Whampoa in 1969.

Having obtained such a high price for the ship, and in view of the highly cyclical state of the shipping industry, the directors decided to dispose of the company. Thus the share capital was sold, and the new directors although operating a 1,290 gross ton vessel for a few years wound up the company in the early 1960s. At this time the firm's offices were situated at Baltic House, Mount Stuart Square, Cardiff.

So another well known Cardiff shipowning venture had disappeared.

An interesting feature was the funnel colours of the Claymore Shipping Co. Ltd. Originally a plain black funnel, in the early 1950s they were changed to the colours of the Glamorgan Cricket Club tie, i.e. dark blue with two narrow yellow bands, a clear reflection of J. C. Clay's connection with the club.

FLEET LIST

Name and Period in Fleet	Gross Tons	History
Daybeam (1) 1920-1929	3,023	1920 built by J. Blumer and Co. Ltd., Sunderland; laid down for the Shipping Controller but completed as *Daybeam* for Claymore Shipping Co. Ltd.; 1929 to F. Sainz de Inchaustequi, Spain renamed *Sebastian;* 1933 to Marques del Real Socorro, Spain; 1936 taken over by Gobierno Provisional de Euzkadi and reported as sailing as *Itxas-Alde,* this name never confirmed and by 1940 all reference had been deleted from Lloyd's Register; 1941 to Comercial de Transportes, Spain; 1943 registered under Compania Comercial Maritima de Transportes S.A.; there must have been some German involvement in the vessel as on 24.11.1943 taken over by the Ministry of War Transport at Gibraltar, managers— Euxine Shipping Co. Ltd; 1944 renamed *Empire Tees;* 1950 to Cia Maritima "Tees" S.A. Panama, renamed *Tees;* 1951 Arthur Jurgenthal appointed as manager; 1951 to Shamrock Shipping Co. Ltd. (C. S. Brown), Belfast, renamed *Clonlee;* 1954 to Muzaffer Taviloglu, Yakup Uzuner and Minittin Topcuoglo, Turkey, renamed *Selamet;* 4.4.1968 arrived at Istanbul for breaking up.
Daybreak (1) 1920-1924	3,102	1920 built by Craig, Taylor and Co. Ltd., Stockton; laid down as *War Temple* for the Shipping Controller, but completed as *Daybreak* for Claymore Shipping Co. Ltd.; 1924 to Oiya Shoji K.K., Japan, renamed *Aikoku Maru;* 12.1.1937 wrecked off Cape Shakotan, Hokkaido, while on passage from Otaru to Shimidzu with a cargo of coal.
Claymont 1920-1928	2,406	1915 built by Craig, Taylor and Co Ltd., Stockton, as *Porthcawl* for Scarisbrick Steamship Co. Ltd. (Eldridge and Morgan), Cardiff; 1920 to Claymore Shipping Co., Ltd.,

74

Name and Period in Fleet	Gross Tons	History
		renamed *Claymont;* 1928 to D/S A/S Laly (C.T. Gogstad and Company), Oslo, renamed *Loke;* 1950 to Liberian Steamship Corp., Liberia, renamed *Milly.* 1954 restyled as Liberian Steamship Corp., Swestfin; 1956 to Capt, H. Ph. M. Krapp; 1961 to Cia. Nav. General S.A., Liberia, renamed *Generous;* 1962 renamed *Hedia;* 11.4 1962 posted missing while on a voyage from Casablanca to Venice with a cargo of phosphate.
Clayton 1920-1927	2,144	1909 built by Wm. Pickersgill and Sons Ltd., Sunderland, as *Pelica* for Scarisbrick Steamship Co. Ltd. (Eldridge and Morgan), Cardiff; 1920 to Claymore Shipping Co. Ltd., renamed *Clayton;* 1927 to Rederi A/B Arild (J.A. Thore), Sweden, renamed *Mongolia;* 13.8.1940 mined and sunk in the Kieler Bucht, in position 54.30N, 10.30E, while on passage from Gefle to Oslebshausen with a cargo of ore.
Daybreak (2) 1925-1934	3,598	1925 built by R. Thompson and Sons Ltd., Sunderland, as *Daybreak* for Claymore Shipping Co. Ltd.; 1934 to C.E. Embiricos, Greece, renamed *Koumoundouros;* 8.10.1942 torpedoed and sunk by German submarine *U68* South of Cape Town in position 34.10S. 17.07E, while on passage from Rosario to Beira via Table Bay with a cargo of maize; of her crew of 31, five were lost.
Dayrose (1) 1928-1942	4,113	1928 built by R. Thompson and Sons Ltd., Sunderland, as *Dayrose* for Claymore Shipping Co. Ltd.; 14.1.1942 torpedoed and sunk by German submarine *U552* near Cape Race in position 46.32N, 53W, while on passage from St. John's Newfoundland to Halifax; 38 crew lost.
Seringa 1939-1945	4,729	1913 built bt Ropner and Sons Ltd., Stockton, as *Falls City* for Bradford Steamship Co. Ltd. (W. R. Smith and Sons), Cardiff; 1917 transferred to St. Just Steamship Co. Ltd. (W. R. Smith and Sons), Cardiff; 1928 transferred

		to Reardon Smith Line Ltd. (Sir William Reardon Smith and Sons Ltd.), Cardiff; 1929 to South Georgia Co. Ltd. (Chr. Salvesen and Company), Leith, renamed *Seringa;* 1939 to Claymore Shipping Co. Ltd.; 1945 to Basra Steam Shipping Co. Ltd. (Galbraith, Pembroke and Co. Ltd.), London; 1946 to East and West Steamship Company, Bombay, renamed *Firoza;* 10.1960 broken up at Karachi by Dodhy.
Daydawn (1) 1940	4,768	1940 built by Wm Pickersgill and Sons Ltd., Sunderland, as *Daydawn* for Claymore Shipping Co. Ltd.; 21.11.1940 torpedoed and sunk by German submarine *U103* in position 56.30N,14.10W, while on passage from Barry to Rio Santiago with a cargo of coal as part of convoy OB244; of her crew of 38, two were lost.
Daybeam (2) 1947-1952	7,233	1944 built by Bethlehem Fairfield Shipyard Inc., Baltimore, as *Samdonard* for the United States War Shipping Administration and bareboat chartered to the Ministry of War Transport, managers—McCowen and Gross Ltd.; 1947 to Claymore Shipping Co. Ltd., renamed *Daybeam;* 1952 to Isla Malvina Cia. Nav. S.A. Panama, renamed *Krioneri;* 1952 to Extramar Panama S.A., Panama, renamed *Alba;* 1961 to Arisona Argentina S.A.; Argentina; 1961 to Plamar S.A., Liberia, renamed *Albamar;* 1962 to Albamar Compania Uruguaya de Nav. S.A., Uruguay; 1964 to Extramar Panama S.A., Liberia, renamed *Albaran;* 23.3.1968 arrived at Kaohsiung for breaking up.
Daydawn (2) 1949-1954	7,036	1943 built by Harland and Wolff Ltd., Glasgow, as *Empire Nerissa* for Ministry of War Transport, managers—Chellew Navigation Co. Ltd., 1946 managers changed to Johnston Warren Lines Ltd.; 1949 to Claymore Shipping Co. Ltd., renamed *Daydawn;* 1954 to Steamship "Induna" Co.

Name and Period in Fleet	Gross Tons	History
		Ltd (Maclay and McIntyre Ltd.), Glasgow, renamed *Loch Don;* 1959 to Maritenia Shipping Co. Ltd. (Kvarnerska Plovidba), Yugoslavia, renamed *Kraljevica;* owners later incorporated into Jugoslavenska Linijksa Plovidba (Yogoslav Line); 24.6.1966 arrived at Split for breaking up by Brodospas.
Dayrose (2) 1953-1956	7,265	1943 built by Permanente Metals Corp. (Shipyard No. 2), Richmond., Cal., as *Mary M. Dodge* for the United States War Shipping Administration; 1943 to Royal Netherlands Government, renamed *Molengraaf;* 1947 to Maats Zeetransport, Netherlands, renamed *Prins Willem II;* 1949 Anthony Veder and Company appointed as managers; 1950 to Maats Zeetransport N.V. (Oranje Line), (A. Veder and Company), Netherlands; 1953 to Claymore Shipping Co. Ltd., renamed *Dayrose;* 1956 to Soc. de Nav. Albion S.A., Panama, renamed *Areti S;* 1963 to Phoebus D. Kyprianou, Lebanon, renamed *Dimos;* 1969 broken up at Whampoa, China.

THE FAIRWATER SHIPPING CO. LTD

Name and Period in Fleet	Gross Tons	History
Fairwater 1928-1945	4,108	1928 built by R. Thompson and Sons Ltd., Sunderland, as *Fairwater* for Fairwater Shipping Co. Ltd.; 4.7.1940 bombed and gunned by German aircraft South East of Start Point in position 50.16N, 02.14W, returned to service after repairs; 1945 to Basra Steam Shipping Co. Ltd. (Galbraith, Pembroke and Co. Ltd), London, renamed *Sherborne;* 1948 to Cereal Trade and Shipping Co. Ltd. (J. D. McLaren and Company), London, renamed *Goose Point;* 1950 to Ellangowan Shipping Co. Ltd. (J. S. McLaren and Company), London; 1951 to Cia. de Vapores Realma S.A., Panama, renamed *Realma;* 1955 to Union Meridianam de Navegacion S.A., Panama, renamed *Charo;* 14.7.1959 arrived at Ghent for breaking up by Van Heyghen Freres.

SHIPS MANAGED ON BEHALF OF THE MINISTRY OF WAR TRANSPORT

Name and Period Managed	Gross Tons	History
Soborg 1940-1945	1,993	1924 built by Wm. Gray and Co. Ltd., West Hartlepool, as *Soborg* for A/S D/S Dannebrog (C. K. Hansen), Denmark; 9.4.1940 while on passage from Denmark to Casablanca in ballast, put into Lisbon and entered British Service; 10.7.1940 taken over by the Ministry of War Transport, managers—Claymore Shipping Co. Ltd.; on D-Day she was present off Northern France; 1945 handed back to her original owners; 1948 to Det Dansk-Norske Dampskibsselskab A/S (R. A. Robbert), Copenhagen renamed *Hamlet;* 1956 to Poseidon Schiffahrt G.m.b.H. (Carl Oestreich), Hamburg; 1957 renamed *Rugard;* 1960 to Compania Marcielo Naviera S.A. (Lemos and Pateras Ltd., London), Beirut, renamed *Agia Trias;* 1965/66 management of owning company taken over by Arcadis Bros. Shipping Corp. (Capt. Michael Arcadis), Piraeus; 10.3.1966 As last ship in a Northbound convoy in the Suez Canal on a voyage from Aqaba to Yugoslavia with a cargo of phosphate the vessel exceeded regulation speed and as there was a strong stern current, she came close to the ship ahead and had to slow down, but her main engine didn't reply due to some failure. While the vessel was manoeuvering to make fast she fell across the canal and hit the canal side. Vessel damaged her propeller and broke her stern frame and rudder. Completely out of command, she drifted with the current and collided with a military ferry-boat, a Suez Canal ferry-boat and several smaller craft. She was towed back to Suez by the Suez Canal tug *Shahm,* where she sank 10.1966 taken over by Mr. Hosni Bur,

Name and Period Managed	Gross Tons	History
		Cairo, but he had difficulties in moving the vessel as the Egyptian army had put in claims for damage to bridges and military installations. Summer 1972 the vessel was still in Suez and was being used as an Army Base for bombing activities by the Arabs; No other details.
Empire Sky 1941-1942	7,455	1941 built by J. L. Thompson and Sons Ltd., Sunderland, as *Empire Sky* for the Ministry of War Transport, managers—Claymore Shipping Co. Ltd.; 14.11.1942 torpedoed and sunk by German submarine *U625* while on a an independent sailing Hull, Loch Ewe and Reykjavik to Archangel with government stores; entire crew lost.

PART 5

LOVERING'S COASTERS

LOVERING AND SONS LTD., CARDIFF

John Samuel George Lovering, the son of a master mariner, was born at Bristol in 1887. His father had invented and patented a navigational aid known as the "Joosi Chart", and in his youth John spent much time demonstrating and selling this in ports throughout the United Kingdom.

Eventually the family moved to Cardiff, which was the undisputed leading coal exporting port in the world, and in 1906 John took the opportunity of joining the existing partnership of Barker and James, coal factors, at Cardiff. Thereafter the business was known as Barker, James and Lovering. Although based at Cardiff, they specialised in the Irish trade, dealing with coal from the Point of Ayr Colliery, North Wales, and from the Forest of Dean, Gloucestershire. This involved the time-chartering of small coasters for the transporting of these cargoes from Point of Ayr and Lydney to Irish Ports. The Point of Ayr's own steam coasters *Tanlan, Talacre* and *Point of Ayr* were often under charter to the partners for this purpose.

Eventually Mr James withdrew from the partnership which was then reconstituted as Barker and Lovering Ltd with offices at Dowlais Chambers, West Bute Street, Cardiff. They owned a considerable number of railway coal wagons, and at premises at Waterloo Wharf, Newport, operated a wagon repairing business under the title of Barker and Lovering Wagon Repairs Ltd.

Mr. Lovering married Amy Horwood during 1913 and they subsequently had six children—Claire, Robert George, Thomas Stanley, Arthur Horwood, Peter Hugh and Paul Alan. In the 1930s following the death of Mr. M. A. Barker, two of Mr Lovering's sons, Robert and Thomas, joined the business. Robert had previously trained as an engineer at Cardiff Docks while Thomas joined the firm straight from school.

The trade in coal to Ireland had expanded and involved the time-chartering of a considerable amount of tonnage, and as a result Mr Lovering decided to enter shipowning on his own account. In consequence in 1936 a new company, Lovering and Sons Ltd. was formed to own and manage ships. The first ship was acquired in 1936 from the Bowles Sand and Gravel, Co. Ltd., of Cardiff. This vessel, a motor coaster of 212 gross tons, had been built as the *Eems* for J. Kostea Nnz. Schpsw. of Giltea for Coenraad Bros., of Rotterdam, and had originally been managed by J. Hof. In 1935 she had passed to the ownership of P. B. de Vries of Delfzijl, for whom she traded as the *Alcyon,* but in 1936 she sank in the Thames Estuary. Subsequently she was raised and sold to Bowles who brought her around to Cardiff and repaired her at Hill's Dry Dock.

Purchased from Bowles she was renamed *Calyx* and thus introduced the firm's well known system of naming ships after plants or parts of plants. Lovering and Sons Ltd. placed the *Calyx* in the trade to Ireland, and so successful was the venture that an order was placed for the construction of a second vessel with E. J. Smit and Zoon, of Westerbroek. This ship, a motor coaster of 290 gross tons, was completed during 1937 and was named *Teasel*.

The following year another new vessel, the *Cornel* (353 gross tons) was delivered to the firm from the yard of E. J. Smit and Zoon, Westerbroek. With the arrival of this new ship the *Calyx* after two years in the fleet was disposed of. She passed to R. Gardner of Lancaster, and on February 3, 1941 she was damaged by a mine eight miles North East of the Bar Light Vessel, in Liverpool Bay. Subsequently repaired, she continued trading for R. Gardner, whose firm was in 1948 restyled as Robert Gardner (Luneside) Ltd. In the 1960s she passed to Continental Cargoes Ltd. of London, and in 1967 was sold to W. T. Bateman, also of London. The following year she was again sold to Southwold Marine Aggregates Ltd., London and in 1971 passed to Carter and Ward of Wickford Ltd., of Wickford, Essex. In 1972 she was bought by Mr. G. W. G. Swift of Maldon, having retained the name *Calyx* throughout. However on March 21, 1973 she sank at the entrance to Ipswich Docks. On August 3 of that same year, she was raised but was so badly damaged that she was declared a constructive total loss, and was broken up at Ipswich.

Thus by 1938 after only two years as shipowners, Lovering and Sons Ltd owned two modern Dutch built motor coasters, the *Teasel* and *Cornel*. While they were principally employed in carrying coal from Lydney and North Wales to Ireland, they occasionally brought cargo homewards. At this time the firm moved their offices to Empire House, Mount Stuart Square, Cardiff, but unfortunately Mr Lovering's second son, Thomas Stanley Lovering died at this time.

At the outbreak of the Second World War Lovering's still owned two ships, which were subsequently operated in the general coastal trades under the directions of the Ministry of War Transport. In 1940 the Ministry appointed the firm to manage the Dutch flag motor coaster *Tromp* (391 gross tons) which dated from 1932, on their behalf.

The following year the firm acquired an additional ship, the *Kindiesel* (339 gross tons) from P. MacCallum and Sons Ltd., Greenock. This vessel had been built at Ardrossan in 1936 and entered the Lovering fleet without change of name. With the arrival of this ship the fleet managed by Lovering and Sons amounted to four vessels.

It is interesting to note that Robert, having trained as an engineer, served aboard the firm's own ships in that capacity throughout the war. His place in the Cardiff office being taken by Arthur who entered the business early in the war. Fortunately they did not suffer any losses through enemy action, and in 1945 the *Tromp* was returned to her original Dutch owners.

Gradually they resumed the peacetime pattern of trade, and the *Teasel, Cornel* and *Kindiesel* were again to be seen unloading coal at Irish ports. However the carriage of coal across the Irish Sea passed to larger vessels and the Lovering fleet became more and more involved with the general coastal trades, carrying varying cargoes which included grain, fertiliser, timber and coal, within the hometrade limits of Elbe/Brest during the winter months, but extending to include the Baltic and Bay of Biscay in the summer.

The coal business of Barker and Lovering Ltd. based at Cardiff, and the wagon repairing business of Barker and Lovering Wagon Repairs Ltd. based at Newport, gradually got back to normal, but the general pattern of this changed following the war, and the subsequent nationalisation of the collieries and railways. During 1946 John Samuel George Lovering died, but by this time his sons, Robert and Arthur, were in a position to take charge of the various commercial interests.

By 1950 the coal trade to Ireland had virtually ended as far as Lovering and Sons Ltd. were concerned, but their interests in the coastal trade expanded to such an extent that in 1947 they decided to acquire a fourth vessel. This ship of 321 gross tons was the *Empire Punch* which had been built in 1942 at Lowestoft for the Ministry of War Transport. She joined the Lovering fleet without change of name. Thus at this time the fleet comprised of the following vessels:

Name	Year Built	Gross Tons
Teasel	1937	290
Cornel	1938	353
Kindiesel	1936	339
Empire Punch	1942	321

Tragically on January 6, 1948 the firm suffered their first marine loss when the *Teasel* when on passage from Belfast to Manchester with a cargo of steel bars, foundered in heavy weather with the loss of all hands.

Late in 1948 the firm acquired a replacement in the form of the *Fennel* (402 gross tons). This ship had been built in 1941 at Hessle as the *Empire Isle* to the order of the Ministry of War Transport, and in 1945 had passed to Comben, Longstaff and Co. Ltd., of London, as the *Suffolkbrook,* for whom she traded for three years before her sale to Lovering and Sons Ltd.

During 1949 a fifth vessel was added to the fleet. This ship, of 512 gross tons, had been built at New Orleans in 1943 as the United States Navy supply vessel *FS136.* In 1948 she passed to commercial owners in Costa

Rica with the name *Dopey*, and in the Lovering fleet she became the *Staniel*. She was an unusual looking ship, in that she had a very heavy mast which had been used to facilitate heavy lifts for the United States Navy. Thus in 1949 the fleet comprised the following vessels:—

Name	Year Built	Gross Tons
Cornel	1938	353
Kindiesel	1936	339
Empire		
Punch	1942	321
Fennel	1941	402
Staniel	1943	512

At about this time Peter Hugh Lovering joined the business as a chief engineer aboard the firm's own ships. He had trained as a marine engineer with the Mount Stuart Dry Dock Co. Ltd., at Cardiff and during the Second World War had served in the Merchant Navy. The youngest son, Paul Alan Lovering, never joined the firm. He trained in marine insurance and is a leading average adjuster. The only daughter, Claire, is living in Canada.

In 1951 the *Kindiesel* was disposed of, passing to the Norwegian flag as the *Sletter*, and in 1956 was again sold and renamed *Sanator*. Her place in the fleet was taken by the motor coaster *Petertown* (528 gross tons) which was acquired from Pinch and Simpson of London. She was Dutch built and dated from 1938. Thus the company were well placed to take full advantage of the post war boom in freight rates.

However, during 1952 the *Fennel* after four years in the fleet was disposed of to the Hindlea Shipping Co. Ltd., of Cardiff, a company in which Mr. John Hindmarsh, a former marine superintendent of Lovering and Sons Ltd. was involved. She traded thereafter as the *Hindlea*, being lengthened in 1954, and survived until on October 27, 1959 when she was wrecked at Moelfre Point, Anglesey, while sheltering on passage from Weston Point to Newport.

During 1953 the company decided to have the *Staniel* lengthened, thus increasing her gross tonnage from 512 to 628, making her the largest vessel ever owned by the firm. At the same time her rather ugly main mast was removed, and a further deck added to her accommodation improving her appearance considerably.

During the next few years the fleet of four ships traded profitably, but by 1956 it was decided to dispose of the *Empire Punch*. She was sold to T. G. Irving Ltd., of Sunderland, becoming the *Oakdene*, and in the 1960s passed without change of name to Sealy's of Sunderland, for whom she served for many years.

In 1956 the firm's headquarters was moved to 1, Mount Stuart, Square, Cardiff.

Gradually falling freight rates caused the firm to sell the *Cornel* in 1957. She went to Thomas Rose and Company of Sunderland as the *Glenside*, and in 1965 passed to Greek interests who renamed her *Michael A.* In 1975 she was resold still under the Greek flag, serving thereafter as the *Elenitsa K.*

On June 27, 1959 the *Staniel* was beached South of Lowestoft with a fire in her cargo of straw while on passage from Boston to Jersey. Two days later, the fire having been extinguished she was refloated and towed to Lowestoft, where following the discharge of her cargo it was found that she was too badly damaged to be worthy of repair. Consequently during October 1959 she was sold for breaking up in Holland.

Due to continuing poor freight rates Lovering and Sons Ltd. decided to withdraw from shipowning altogether, and at the same time as the sale of the damaged *Staniel,* the last ship *Peterstown* was sold, passing to Italian owners as the *Sirenella.*

The businesses of Barker and Lovering Ltd., coal factors, and Barker and Lovering Wagon Repairs Ltd. continued trading under the general directions of Robert and Arthur Lovering, who also owned the Uskside Filling Station, at Mill Parade, Newport. However, in the late 1960s these interests were disposed of. Barker and Lovering Ltd. was sold to the Evans and Reid Coal Co. Ltd., of Empire House, Mount Stuart Square, Cardiff.

Robert died during 1979, but Arthur became a director of Braithwaite, Heslop and Co. Ltd., coal factors, a subsidiary of the Evans and Reid Coal Co. Ltd. Peter was involved in business on his own account trading as Lovering Fuel Oils Ltd., with offices still at 1, Mount Stuart Square, Cardiff.

Thus yet another of the small South Wales family shipping businesses had come to an end.

FLEET LIST

Name and Period in Fleet	Gross Tons	History
Calyx 1936-1938	212	1929 built by J. Kostea. Hnz. Schpsw. Giltea, Groningen, as *Eems* for Coenraad Bros. (J. Hof), Rotterdam; 1935 to P. B. de Vries, Delfzijl, renamed *Alcyon;* 1936 sank in the Thames Estuary, but subsequently raised; 1936 to Bowles Sand and Gravel Co. Ltd., Cardiff; and repaired at Hill's Dry Dock, Cardiff; 1936 to Lovering and Sons Ltd., renamed *Calyx;* 1938 to R. Gardner, Lancaster; 3.2.1941 damaged by a mine 8 miles North East of the Bar Light Vessel, Liverpool Bay, later repaired and returned to service; 1948 owners restyled as Robert Gardner (Luneside) Ltd.; 1960s to Continental Cargoes Ltd., London 1967 to W. T. Bateman, London; 1968 to Southwold Marine Aggregates Ltd., London 1971 to Carter and Ward of Wickford Ltd., Wickford; 1972 to G. W. G. Swift, Maldon; 21.3.1973 sank at the entrance to Ipswich Docks; 3.8.1973 raised but declared a constructive total loss; 1973/74 broken up at Ipswich.
Teasel 1937-1948	290	1937 built by E. J. Smit and Zoon, Westerbroek, as *Teasel* for Lovering and Sons Ltd.; 6.1.1948 foundered with all hands off Maughold Head, Isle of Man, while on passage Belfast to Manchester with a cargo of steel bars.
Cornel 1938-1957	353	1938 built by E. J. Smit and Zoon, Westerbroek, as *Cornel* for Lovering and Sons Ltd.; 1957 to Thomas Rose and Company, Sunderland, renamed *Glenside;* 1965 to G. and M. Amiridakis and Company, Piraeus, renamed Michael A; 1975 to A. Kokkinidi and others, Greece, renamed *Elenitsa K;* No other details.

Name and Period in Fleet	Gross Tons	History
Kindiesel 1941-1951	339	1936 built by Androssan Dockyard Ltd., Ardrossan, as *Kindiesel* for Kindiesel Shipping Co. Ltd. (P. MacCallum and Sons Ltd), Greenock; 1941 to Lovering and Sons Ltd.; 1951 to Skibs A/S Karlander (Egil Paulsen), Fredrikstad, renamed *Sletter;* 1956 to Partrederiet Senator (Gunnar Aarseth), Alesund, Norway, renamed *Senator;* 1969 no other details.
Empire Punch 1947-1955	321	1942 built by Richards Ironworks Ltd., Lowestoft, as *Empire Punch* for the Ministry of War Transport, managers—Hannan Samuel and Co. Ltd.; 1944 management transferred to Argosies Ltd.; 1947 to Lovering and Sons Ltd.; 1955 to T. G. Irving Ltd., Sunderland, renamed *Oakdene;* 1960s to G.I.F. and E. C. D. Sealy, Sunderland; no other details.
Fennel 1948-1952	402	1941 built by Henry Scarr Ltd., Hessle, as *Empire Isle* for the Ministry of War Transport, managers—Free Trade Wharf Co. Ltd., Hull; 1942 management transferred to Comben, Longstaff and Co. Ltd., London; 1945 to Comben, Longstaff and Co. Ltd., London, renamed *Suffolkbrook;* 1948 to Lovering and Sons Ltd., renamed *Fennel;* 1952 to Hindlea Shipping Co. Ltd., Cardiff, renamed *Hindlea;* 1954 lengthened and deepened by Elsflether Werft, Elsfleth, gross tonnage increased to 506; 27.10.1959 wrecked at Moelfre Point, Anglesey, while sheltering on passage from Weston Point to Newport; her crew of eight saved.
Staniel 1949-1959	512	1943 built by Higgins Industries Inc., New Orleans, as *FS136* for the United States Navy; 1948 to Cia. Sao Marco, Costa Rica, renamed *Dopey;* 1949 to Lovering and Sons Ltd., renamed *Staniel;* 1953 lengthened, gross tonnage increased to 628; 27.6.1959 beached on fire South of Lowestoft, while on passage from Boston, Lincs. to Jersey with a cargo of straw; 28.6.1959 fire extinguished 29.6.1959 refloated,

Name and Period in Fleet	Gross Tons	History
		but declared a constructive total loss; 10.1959 broken up at Ymuiden, Holland.
Petertown 1951-1959	528	1938 built by N. V. Schpsw. Gebr. van der Werf., Deest, as *Petertown* for Pinch and Simpson, London; 1951 to Lovering and Sons Ltd.; 1959 to Giusto Camalie C., Leghorn, Italy, renamed *Sirenella;* 1978 no other details.

SHIP MANAGED ON BEHALF OF THE MINISTRY OF WAR TRANSPORT

Name and Period Managed	Gross Tons	History
Tromp 1940-1945	391	1932 built N.V. Industrieele Maats De Noord, Alblasserdam, as *Flying Irishman* for N. V. Motorzeevaart Maats "Mozem" (N. V. W. H. James and Company's Scheep. and Handel Maats), Rotterdam; 1938 management transferred to N. V. J. Vermaas' Scheepvaartbedrijf, renamed *Tromp;* 1939 to Reed "De Noord", same managers; 27.5.1940 time-chartered by the Ministry of War Transport, managers—Freight Express Ltd.; 1940 management transferred to Lovering and Sons Ltd., vessel remained under the Dutch flag throughout the war; 12.7.1945 returned to original owners; 8.12.1946 mined and sunk South of Langeland, in position 54.39N, 10.45E, while on passage from Holtenau to Rotterdam.